U0745368

The MACAT Library
世界思想宝库钥匙丛书

解析伯顿·G.马尔基尔

《漫步华尔街》

AN ANALYSIS OF

BURTON G. MALKIEL'S

A RANDOM WALK DOWN WALL STREET

Nick Burton ◎ 著

刘积慧 ◎ 译

上海外语教育出版社
外教社 SHANGHAI FOREIGN LANGUAGE EDUCATION PRESS

MACAT

目　录

CONTENTS

引 言

要 点

- 伯顿·G.马尔基尔是一位美国学者和投资人，最初在华尔街担任分析师，之后转战学术界，学术事业十分成功。
- 《漫步华尔街》认为，股票*市场价格的走势完全不可预测，是"随机的"*。
- 《漫步华尔街》支持有效市场假说*。该假说认为，没有投资者能够始终"战胜市场"，因为在当今世界，全部投资者几乎能立刻得知所有能影响股票价格的合法信息。

伯顿·G.马尔基尔其人

伯顿·G.马尔基尔，《漫步华尔街：股市历久弥新的成功投资策略》（1973）一书的作者，1932年出生于波士顿，是美国著名的经济学家、投资人、商人和作家。马尔基尔最初在华尔街担任分析师，不久转入学术界，获普林斯顿大学经济学*博士学位，并留在普林斯顿经济系任教。结束了在普林斯顿大学杰出的学术生涯之后，马尔基尔现任汉华银行经济学讲席荣退教授（"荣退"意为荣誉退休）。

在从事学术研究的同时，马尔基尔也活跃在商界；他曾任十几家私营企业的董事，美国白宫经济顾问委员会（专为美国总统提供咨询的机构）委员，以及美国金融协会*主席。

尽管马尔基尔在学界和商界有诸多专业成就，但他最为人所知的仍是《漫步华尔街》一书。该书自1973年问世以来即成为畅销书，现已再版11次。

《漫步华尔街》的出版将马尔基尔推到了风口浪尖。专业投资人士能否预测股市走势引发了热议，自此马尔基尔一直处于这场争论的中心。他出版发表了多部投资理论和实践的书籍和文章，还根据《漫步华尔街》的结论创立或声援现实生活中的投资产品（投资者可以投资的基金等）。

《漫步华尔街》的主要内容

《漫步华尔街》是一部关于股票市场——主要是美国股市——的著作，该书认为股票价格的变化是完全随机的。该观点将作者马尔基尔与华尔街的传统观念及其一众"专家"对立起来（"专家"这个术语用在金融服务领域——银行、保险公司、投资基金等——只会招来马尔基尔的嘲讽）。这些专家声称，他们可以预测股市未来的表现，即股票的价格变化。《漫步华尔街》直接、有力地反驳了这种观点："股票价格的短期变化是不可预测的。投资咨询服务、收益预测和复杂的图表模型毫无用处。"[1]

在某种程度上，这种市场"随机"论肯定了华尔街的效率*。马尔基尔认为，炒股的人竞争太过激烈，谁也没有真正的优势。有太多人在收集和传播可能影响股票价格的信息，因而不存在可以让人"稳操胜券"的（合法）秘密。所有秘密都已经公之于众——除非是内幕交易*（根据机密信息来买卖股票，例如公司计划扩大，或计划公布不良收益），而这是非法的。

因此，马尔基尔认为，每一只股票当前的价格完全反映了当前有关公司价值的所有可知信息。这种观点，即有效市场假说，通常被称为随机漫步理论*。

有效市场假说认为，每当市场上出现新信息，可以让人具备真正"优势"时（能赶在其他投资者之前预测某只股票是会上涨还是下跌），该信息会迅速传播开来。没有哪一方能够单独从中获利。某投资者可能会（合法地）先于他人片刻收到新信息，从而完成一笔出色的投资，但长远来看，这种策略并不会持续奏效；这是因为股市"善于根据新信息进行自我调整，没人能以优于市场的方式预测未来走向。由于专业人士有所举动，单只股票的价格很快便能反映所有可获取的信息"。[2]

那么，如果股市里每一只股票真的只是个赌局（仅仅是运气问题），那么人们该如何投资呢？

有一点似乎是肯定的：股票市场本身的价值。几十年来，尽管股市跌宕起伏（上下波动），但股市市值显著上升。马尔基尔推荐一种"买入并持有"的策略，选取各类股票形成投资组合（即一篮子股票），使投资组合的整体表现拟合股市的平均水平。长期来看，这种投资似乎肯定会带来可观的回报。既然无法战胜市场，那就最好相信市场本身。这种说法本身十分激进——也是华尔街专业人士最不希望"普通投资者"去做的。

《漫步华尔街》的学术价值

马尔基尔的观点自 1973 年问世以来，表现出了非凡的持久力。对公众来说，《漫步华尔街》在知识层面挑战了专业理财经理人的价值。理财经理人不仅不可能始终如一地战胜市场，而且在每次买卖客户股票时还会收取高昂的服务费和交易手续费。因此，即使《漫步华尔街》再版了 11 次，金融服务业的许多专业人士仍想推翻书中的结论。然而，任何对股市有兴趣的人都必须面对该书的结论。尽管招来了反对声，该书仍广受投资专业人士、金融理论家和"普通投资者"的欢迎。赢得最后这批人的青睐是一项了不起的成就，因为"普通投资者"经常被承诺帮助他们"战胜市场"的投资大佬们牢牢掌控。

马尔基尔在 11 个版本中都一直坚持认为，**没人能长期战胜市场**。理财经理人的总体业绩与股市本身表现的数据证实了他的说法。所以他的论点仍一如既往地站住了脚跟。在首次出版四十余年后，《漫步华尔街》仍经常被财经媒体和投资理论学者引述和谈及，也常受到华尔街专业人士的抨击。

学生阅读《漫步华尔街》，会接触到投资理论和实践的基本问题：股票价格如何变化？为什么变化？真的有人能"战胜市场"吗？如果不能，普通投资者应当怎么做？如马尔基尔所言："关于股市有太多扑朔迷离的说法，需要一本书来正本清源。"[3]

《漫步华尔街》甚至（或专门）向非专业人士普及金融知识。马尔基尔旨在"为个人投资者提供可读性强的投资指南"。[4]金融界在过去四十年里变得更加复杂。投资基金现在使用的各种金融工具令人眼花缭乱。从技术上讲，这些工具可以是任何一种可交易的资产（包括现金），甚至可以是公司或个人持有的债务。马尔基尔的这本书是一个清晰中肯的指南，引导投资者在这个扑朔迷离的金融界里辨明方向。

四十多年来，《漫步华尔街》一直备受追捧和争议。不论马尔基尔的观点是否正确，可以说，他已经成功实现了《漫步华尔街》的目标——让专业人士和普通投资者都仔细斟酌"不能战胜市场"这一观点。

1. 伯顿·G.马尔基尔:《漫步华尔街:股市历久弥新的成功投资策略》,纽约:W.W.诺顿公司,2015年,第26页。
2. 马尔基尔:《漫步华尔街》,第190页。
3. 马尔基尔:《漫步华尔街》,第18页。
4. 马尔基尔:《漫步华尔街》,第19页。

第一部分：学术渊源

1 作者生平与历史背景

要点 🔑

- 《漫步华尔街》的分析基础是有效市场假说，通常被称为随机漫步理论，这一理论认为股票价格的波动是不可预测的。

- 《漫步华尔街》结合了马尔基尔对投资理论的学术理解及其专业金融知识。

- 有效市场假说挑战了盛行且通常十分昂贵的投资策略，引发了激烈的争论——尤其引起了那些通过自称知道如何战胜市场来牟利的投资专业人士的热议。

为何要读这部著作？

伯顿·G.马尔基尔的《漫步华尔街：股市历久弥新的成功投资策略》首次出版于 1973 年，如今已再版 11 次，共售出 150 万册。该书推崇有效市场假说——即股市十分高效（公司的所有可知信息都反映在股票价格中），未来的（不可知的）价格波动无法预测——并已成为投资领域的经典文献。马尔基尔是学术界和金融界的领军人物。他有个著名观点："市场对股票的定价非常有效，以至于一只蒙住眼睛的猴子在股票列表上投镖，都可以选出媲美专家管理的投资组合。"[1]（"投资组合"指为投资者谋取收益而选取的股票组合。）

书中宣扬的有效市场假说认为，证券*价格能捕捉到有关公司的所有新闻和信息。"证券"通常指股票或债券等：证明对某上市公司具有部分所有权的金融合同（股票），或是对公司或政府机构贷款的偿付承诺（债券）。如果股票价格并未反映所有可知的信息，则该股票定价不当（即低效）。根据有效市场假说，人们便会蜂拥而至利用这种不平衡（通过买入或卖出定价不当的股票），直至这种低效现象消失。而纠正低效现象的过程快得几乎在瞬息之间，因而要长期利用这种低效现象来赚钱几乎是不可能的。

根据这一理论，马尔基尔提出投注于市场本身：通过购买众多公司的股票形成分散化的投资组合（持有的股票），使投资组合的价值与整个股市价值相匹配。这种投资组合叫"指数基金"*，具有管理费低和组合周转率低的特点——只需向专业人士支付很少的管理费和交易手续费。[2] 这一简单得令人难以置信的策略长期来看几乎总是胜过华尔街（纽约市金融区或泛指美国货币市场）高明的共同基金经理的业绩。

"共同基金"*是指投资者共同持有、并交由专业投资人士管理的分散的股票组合。共同基金经理总是谋求自身利益最大化，不断地买入和卖出投资组合中的股票——收取高昂的费用，并产生需要由客户来承担的资本利得税*（股票升值部分需缴纳的税）。

> "我一直是个投资者，并且是个成功的市场参与者。究竟有多成功，我是不会说的，因为学术界有一种奇特现象，就是认为教授不应该赚钱。"
>
> —— 伯顿·G.马尔基尔:《漫步华尔街》

作者生平

马尔基尔 1932 年出生于波士顿，毕业于著名的波士顿拉丁学校，而后就读于哈佛大学，1953 年获得学士学位，1955 年获工商管理硕士学位。在美国陆军金融军团服役后，马尔基尔在前华尔街投资公司史密斯巴尼公司（现已并入摩根斯坦利财富管理公司）做了两年副经理。

1960 年，马尔基尔从华尔街转战学术界，获美国顶级学府之一普林斯顿大学的经济学博士学位。他随后留在普林斯顿大学担任助理教授，很快升任讲座教授（最高学术职务）和经济系主任。对马尔基尔来说，进入学术界是解锁更优投资策略的关键。

这一转型使他与华尔街的前同事们分道扬镳。华尔街的同事们认为："高校教师沉迷于各种方程式和希腊符号（更不用说乏味的散文了），不辨牛熊（在股市术语里，'牛市'乐观，价格看涨；'熊市'悲观，价格看跌），哪怕在最显而易见的情况下也看不出二者的差别。"[3] 然而，马尔基尔在此期间还兼任了好些公司的董事。

这种横跨商界和学术界的双重身份使马尔基尔成为一位不寻常的（而且异常成功的）人物。1981 年马尔基尔担任耶鲁大学组织与管理学院院长，最后他又回到了普林斯顿，成为汉华银行经济学讲席教授，这也是他现在保有的荣誉（退休）学术头衔。

创作背景

在《漫步华尔街》一书中，马尔基尔提出了一个明确的核心问题：所有公司股票的走势是可预测的，还是完全随机的？

如果证券价格确实捕捉到了各个公司的全部新闻和信息，则未来的价格路径只能是随机的，因为价格完全依赖于未来的新闻："如果一则新闻并非随机，也就是说，如果该新闻依赖于较早的一则新闻，那它根本就不是什么新闻了。"[4]

由于横跨商界和学术界，马尔基尔对两者的运作方式有着独到的见解。在《漫步华尔街》一书中，他抨击两者都掩盖了市场（在他眼里）的简单真相：市场遵循有效市场假说，因而投资股市无异于"随机漫步"。从这个意义上说，马尔基尔的观点在投资界和投资理论与研究领域的学术界都是独一无二的。

马尔基尔在这两个圈子里都圈粉无数，他曾在先锋集团 * 担任董事逾 30 年。先锋集团是一个低费率的指数基金投资集团，现在管理着超过 3 万亿美元的资产。正如马尔基尔在《漫步华尔街》中所写，自从 2007—2008 年金融崩溃 *（由高风险的美国房地产市场崩盘和相关金融机构的投资亏损引发的事件）以来，投资者愈发认同他的简单策略："2014 年，个人和机构投资者约有三分之一的资金投向了指数基金。而且这个比例还在上升。"[5]

虽然马尔基尔现已退休，但他仍然是个多产的学者。

1. 伯顿·G.马尔基尔：《漫步华尔街：股市历久弥新的成功投资策略》，纽约：W. W. 诺顿公司，2015 年，第 19 页。
2. 马尔基尔：《漫步华尔街》，第 383 页。
3. 马尔基尔：《漫步华尔街》，第 26 页。
4. 马尔基尔：《漫步华尔街》，第 155 页。
5. 马尔基尔：《漫步华尔街》，第 181 页。

2 学术背景

要点 ⚷━

- 《漫步华尔街》从学术的角度剖析股市，探究我们究竟是否可以预测股市走势。

- 在《漫步华尔街》一书中，马尔基尔质疑了技术分析*和基本面分析*这两种声称能预测股票价格走势的主要方法，也继续质疑了一些新方法。

- 在《漫步华尔街》出版前后，许多经济学家也得出了与马尔基尔相同的结论。

著作语境

伯顿·G.马尔基尔所著的《漫步华尔街：股市历久弥新的成功投资策略》介绍了一种全新的投资分析法，被称为有效市场假说，有时亦被称作随机漫步理论。该书探讨了一个最基本的金融问题——为什么价格在证券市场中会变化。[1]（"证券"是指股票和债券等）该书指出，股票价格反映了所有关于公司价值的可知信息，因此，人们无法利用合法获取的信息来"战胜市场"。

许多投资者试图利用股票价格与股票实际价值之间经常出现的差距。他们试图找出被低估、可望升值的股票——尤其是那些升值空间更大的股票。[2]后者的差距是关键：因为如果投资者挑选出的股票业绩优于他人，则算是"战胜市场"。投资者常常运用令人眼花缭乱的预测技术来追求此类超额回报。[3]然而，有效市场假说认为，没有人能一直保持这种优势。

很少有理论曾引发如此激烈的辩论。例如，著名的哈佛经济学家迈克尔·詹森*曾说过："经济学中没有哪个命题比有效市场假说具有更坚实的实证*（以数据为基础）支撑。"而知名投资者彼得·林奇*则说过："有效市场？那是一堆垃圾，疯狂的玩意。"[4]

> "市场并不总是正确的，甚至常常是错误的。但没有人或机构始终比市场更了解市场。"
>
> —— 伯顿·G.马尔基尔：《漫步华尔街》

学科概览

该学科的基本问题是，是否有方法可以预测股票价格的走势。这自然引起了投资者和学术投资理论家的热议，其中一些人认为股票价格是可预测的，而另一些则认为不可预测。

关于这一问题的主要观点源于两个存在已久的学派："技术分析派"和"基本面分析派"。马尔基尔质疑了两者。

简单说来，技术分析派研究过去的股票价格和交易量，以期预测未来的价格。对于这种方法的追随者而言，市场只有10%取决于逻辑，90%取决于心理*；他们"认为投资是一种预判其他投资者行为的游戏"。[5]

基本面分析派则试图反其道而行之——尽量不受大众的乐观和悲观情绪的影响。这种方法分析财务统计数据，如公司盈利或资产价值，以确定"价值被低估的"股票。[6]

自《漫步华尔街》问世以来，出现了许多新的学派。马尔基尔一直与时俱进，并经常以严谨的学术研究来审视新理论。对于任何方法或"巫术"能真正奏效并"战胜市场"，他仍然持怀疑态度。

学术渊源

1900 年，法国数学家路易·巴舍利耶*发表《投机理论》，提出"投机者*的数学预期是零"。换言之，凡是想投机或试图猜测哪些股票会表现更好的投资者不能指望获利，因为亏损总是与收益扯平。巴舍利耶的研究远远超前，被忽视了五十多年。[7] 在它被重新发现之前，英国经济学家约翰·梅纳德·凯恩斯*和美国经济学家米尔顿·弗里德曼*等理论家一直在研究同样的问题，并得出了类似的结论。

1970 年，美国经济学家尤金·F.法玛*就这个问题发表了一篇言之凿凿的论文。法玛后来获得了诺贝尔经济学奖。他在论文中指出："支持有效市场模型的证据非常多，而且反例很少（这在经济学上实属罕见）。"[8]

随着这些数学分析的出现，越来越多的文献表达了对华尔街专业人士能力的不信任。美国股票经纪人小弗雷德·施韦德*所著的《客户的游艇在哪里？》（1940）是这类文献的早期经典。"遗憾的是，知道任意一种证券持续两年走势的金融专家少得可怜，"施韦德在书中写道，"大多数人在短得多的时间里通常都错得离谱。"[9]

近期的诺贝尔经济学奖得主罗伯特·J.希勒*出版的《非理性繁荣》（2003），批判了市场的"正反馈循环"，即价格上涨诱使更多人买入，进一步推高价格，直到大众心理而非欺诈滋生出一种庞氏骗局*[10]（庞氏骗局中，早期投资者获得高额回报率，但如果没有更多投资者注入资金，欺诈性的骗局就崩溃了，大多数参与者蒙受损失）。经济学家纳西姆·尼古拉斯·塔勒布*的《黑天鹅》（2007）从实证和哲学两方面质疑股票过去的业绩能预测未来表现这一观点。[11]（实证是通过观察可以验证的证据。）

《漫步华尔街》的结论沿袭了批判金融文献的传统。马尔基尔持续的严谨学术研究也为之提供了充分论据。

---

1. 乔纳森·克拉克等："有效市场假说"，罗伯特·C.阿尔法编，《专家财务规划：行业领导者的投资策略》，纽约：约翰威立出版社，2001 年，第 126 页。

2. 克拉克："有效市场假说"，第 126 页。

3. 克拉克："有效市场假说"，第 126 页。

4. 克拉克："有效市场假说"，第 127 页。

5. 伯顿·G.马尔基尔：《漫步华尔街：股市历久弥新的成功投资策略》，纽约：W. W. 诺顿公司，2015 年，第 110 页。

6. 伯顿·G.马尔基尔："有效市场假说及其批评"，《经济展望杂志》第 17 卷，2003 年冬第 1 期，第 59 页。

7. 马丁·塞维尔："有效市场假说的历史"，《伦敦大学学院研究报告》第 11 卷，2011 年第 4 期，第 2 页。

8. 尤金·F.法玛："有效资本市场：理论与实证研究回顾"，《金融学报》第 25 卷，1970 年 5 月第 2 期，第 383 页。

9. 小弗雷德·施韦德：《客户的游艇在哪里？》，霍博肯：约翰威立出版社，2006 年，第 14 页。

10. 罗伯特·J.希勒：《非理性繁荣》，普林斯顿：普林斯顿大学出版社，2000 年，第 64—68 页。

11. 纳西姆·尼古拉斯·塔勒布：《黑天鹅：如何应对不可预知的未来》，伦敦：企鹅出版社，2007 年。

3 主导命题

要点 ⚷

- 美国经济学家尤金·F.法玛 1965 年发表的一篇文章首次将"有效市场"这一现代理念运用于股票交易当中。这在当时是个激进的观点，挑战了整个金融服务业*的价值，也启发了马尔基尔撰写《漫步华尔街》。

- 有效市场假说受到各种理论的抨击。这些理论试图找寻和利用股票价格的变动模式。

- 2007—2008 年的金融崩溃或许是有效市场假说面临的最大挑战。一些人声称这场危机证伪了有效市场假说。

核心问题

伯顿·G.马尔基尔在《漫步华尔街：股市历久弥新的成功投资策略》一书中研究的核心问题有："股票价格为什么会变化？这些变化是如何产生的？有可能预测吗？"事实上，这些问题也是整个金融领域最核心的问题。

虽然从表面上看，这些问题似乎关乎理性和数学，然而情感——尤其是贪婪和恐慌等极端情绪——在股市中的作用是不可低估的。英国经济学家约翰·梅纳德·凯恩斯有个著名的论断，他认为股市的走势源于古怪的心理因素："我们积极行动的很大一部分原因是由于自发的乐观而非数学预期。"[1] 这些活动发自他所谓的"动物本能——一种自发的冲动让人采取行动而非无所作为"。[2] 凯恩斯的结论是："在非理性的世界里寻求理性的投资方法无异灭顶之灾。"[3]

至于股票价格如何变动、为何变动等问题，仍然至关重要，对投资者和整个金融服务业都产生了巨大影响。1945 年第二次世界大战 * 的结束带来了美国经济繁荣的新时代。大量资金涌入股市，金融业迅猛发展，金融专业人士无不承诺为客户谋取超额回报（这显然是不可能的，因为不可能所有人取得的收益都高于平均水平）。自此出现了许多知名的策略，统统承诺能预测股票市场的"未来走势"。

"有效市场"一词首次出现在尤金·F.法玛 1965 年发表的一篇文章中。他在文中提出："在有效市场中，任何时间点的证券的实际价格都很好地估计了其内在的（真实的、核心的）价值。"[4] 有效市场假说的支持者坚称，股票价格波动是无法预测的。然而，这在当时是一个激进的想法，激励了马尔基尔创作《漫步华尔街》，挑战金融服务业及其许多声称对股票价格走势几乎是明察秋毫、远见卓识的分析。

> "一只蒙住眼睛的猴子向股票列表投镖，都可以选出媲美专家精选出的投资组合。"
>
> —— 伯顿·G. 马尔基尔：《漫步华尔街》

参与者

如果说股价波动是由逻辑和情感二者共同驱使的，那么两个最大的预测阵营只关注二者中的一方，或许就不足为奇了。

技术分析派研究过去的价格变动以预测未来的价格走势。他们探寻价格波动的模式。他们认为，投资的情感或心理因素，而不是逻辑，造成了价格的变动。他们研究市场中其他投资者的行为，以预测投资者未来可能的举动。[5] 相反，基本面分析派希望利用股票的"真实价值"，试图找出股票的低估价格（低效）及其真实价值之间的缺口。这两派共同占据了金融服务业的半壁江山。

随着时间的推移，更多有效市场假说的对手出现了。说来也许令人惊讶，这些对手来自学术界，而非商界。其中之一是现代投资组合理论*。该理论主张，风险较高的股票组合如果以恰当的方法分散（与其他股票混合），可以大幅降低风险。另一个对手是行为金融学*，已经成为一个快速发展的学科。行为金融学认为投资者远非理性；该理论专门研究过度自信、判断偏差和羊群心理等行为。该理论认为，对这些因素的洞见能使投资者从股票价格及其真实价值之间的缺口中牟利。

还有大量其他金融投资策略不断涌现，其中好些都不乏追随者。

当代论战

有效市场假说不仅仅是一个观点；就理性而言，有效市场假说对多数金融服务业构成了威胁。既然不可能战胜市场，何必还要尝试？——特别是在管理费用高企，每次买卖股票的交易手续费高昂，以及卖出所有获利的股票都需缴纳较高资本利得税的情况下。

法玛备受推崇的研究论文"有效资本市场：理论与实证研究回顾"（1970）以大量现实世界的研究为有效市场假说提供了支撑。在此后的十年中，这种模式继续在投资者和经济学家中占据主导地位。有效市场假说引领着金融界和学术界，不断有人发表研究表示声援。[6] 然而，到了20世纪80年代和90年代，有效市场假说开始受到学者和商界的质疑。例如，有研究表明，投资者经常对新闻反应过度或反应不足——他们对股票的出价过高或过低。仅凭这一点，至少部分地反驳了有效市场假说。[7]

2007—2008 年的经济崩溃或许是有效市场假说面临的最大挑战。包括亿万富翁对冲基金经理乔治·索罗斯 * 在内的许多人都认为这次危机使有效市场假说名誉扫地。毕竟，由于受到追逐高收益的投资者的不断追捧，某些金融产品，特别是那些与美国次级房地产市场 *（房地产市场上的高风险投资）挂钩的金融产品定价过高。最后，泡沫 *——整体定价过高——破灭，大部分投资都变得毫无价值。

马尔基尔直面 2007—2008 年的房地产崩盘。他说，有效市场假说确实奏效了；市场最终找到了那些投资的正确价格，只是花了几年时间。"明确的结论就是，"马尔基尔坚称，"市场每次都会自我纠正。市场最终会修正一切非理性。"[8]

1. 约翰·梅纳德·凯恩斯：《就业、利息和货币通论》，伦敦：麦克米伦出版社，1936 年，第 161—162 页。
2. 凯恩斯：《就业、利息和货币通论》，第 161—162 页。
3. 米尔顿·弗里德曼和安娜·雅各布森·施瓦茨：《美国货币史（1867—1960）》，普林斯顿：普林斯顿大学出版社，1963 年，第 814 页。
4. 尤金·F. 法玛："有效资本市场：理论与实证研究回顾"，《金融学报》第 25 卷，1970 年 5 月第 2 期，第 383 页。
5. 伯顿·G. 马尔基尔：《漫步华尔街：股市历久弥新的成功投资策略》，纽约：W. W. 诺顿公司，2015 年，第 110—111 页。

6. 拉米·马侯治："金融市场环境"，开放大学，登录日期2015年11月10日，http://www.open.edu/openlearn/money-management/money/accounting-and-finance/the-financial-markets-context/content-section—acknowledgements。

7. 马侯治："金融市场环境"。

8. 马尔基尔：《漫步华尔街》，第104页。

4 作者贡献

要点 🗝️

- 在《漫步华尔街》一书中，马尔基尔罗列了大量的证据和实际交易数据，推翻了各种自称可以超出股票市场平均水平的投资理论。

- 通过将有效市场假说理论转化为现实的投资策略——推行指数基金，投注于整个市场的价值而不是个股价值的上升——马尔基尔对投资界产生了他人难以企及的影响。

- 尽管有效市场假说主要是由诺贝尔经济学奖得主尤金·F.法玛等其他学者提出的，但马尔基尔继续深化了该理论并将之发扬光大。

作者目标

伯顿·G.马尔基尔写作《漫步华尔街：股市历久弥新的成功投资策略》一书的目的十分单纯，令人钦佩。首先，他想证明有效市场假说的有效性，即证券（如股票和债券）的价格能够反映发行证券的公司的所有可知新闻和信息。他收集了大量的数据和证据，包括股票的历史价格，并优雅地呈现出来。马尔基尔的另一目的是逐一反驳有效市场假说的挑战者，特别是长期存在的技术分析派和基本面分析派。他也驳斥了后来兴起的投资策略，例如现代投资组合理论（一种投资者通过选择风险相互抵消的资产使风险最小化的方法）。尽管马尔基尔承认行为金融学（探索市场参与者的心理特征来解释市场动向）的见解很有价值，但他对日益壮大的行为金融学总体持批判态度。"可以想象，"他写道，"这是一个可以发表文章，讲授课程获利，而且撰写毕业论文的全新的领域。"[1]

马尔基尔想要证明，如果考虑到所有"主动式管理"策略（基于频繁买卖股票的策略）的高昂费用、交易成本和税收负担，普通投资者只需依靠市场本身就划算得多——投资由多种股票组成的指数基金，然后静待升值。指数基金是由多种精心挑选出来的股票形成的组合，能反映股票市场的整体业绩水平。

最后，马尔基尔旨在为读者提供一份全面的财务指南。《漫步华尔街》给出了许多对普通投资者有用的财务忠告，从保险、孩子的教育费用，到（合法）避税，一应俱全。

> "我无意向大家承诺创造股票市场的奇迹。事实上，这本书的副标题很可能是'让人稳扎稳打致富的书'。"
>
> —— 伯顿·G.马尔基尔：《漫步华尔街》

研究方法

虽然经济学家尤金·F.法玛常被视为有效市场假说之父，但《漫步华尔街》将有效市场假说的学术研究成果传播给非专业读者。1973年《漫步华尔街》出版后，人们普遍意识到，大多数"主动式管理"的共同基金（大量投资者共同筹集、并交由专业人士代表投资者买卖证券的资金）并未跑赢股市。马尔基尔在《漫步华尔街》第一版中引述有效市场假说理论并呼吁："我们需要的……是管理费用最低的共同基金（投资者无需为买卖股票而付费），只购买数百只构成股票市场平均值的股票，不为跑赢市场而频繁交易。"[2]换言之，他主张"指数共同基金"：广泛分散、业绩与整个股票市场相仿的股票组合。

《漫步华尔街》运用有效市场假说提出了一种非常实用的长期

方法，而这种方法当时在其他地方已有先例。市场理论家约翰·C.博格尔 * 在《漫步华尔街》出版的次年创立了美国投资管理公司先锋集团，并于 1976 年创建了世界上第一只面向普通投资者的指数共同基金。虽然博格尔对这只突破性的指数基金提了很多建议，而且长期关注这种方法，但马尔基尔及《漫步华尔街》将该方法的目标最清晰地呈现在公众眼前。1977 年，马尔基尔加入了先锋集团董事会，任职了 28 年。先锋集团目前是全球最大的共同基金公司之一，管理的资产总额逾 3 万亿美元。虽然先锋集团的开创性指数基金在 1974 年成立之初因不曾试图战胜市场而备受嘲讽，但如今指数共同基金已被视为行业标杆。《漫步华尔街》也成了指数共同基金发展的公认的理论依据。

时代贡献

法玛 1970 年发表突破性的论文"有效资本市场：理论与实证研究回顾"时，证实了其他许多研究者已经思考多时的命题。[3] 例如，博格尔在普林斯顿大学的毕业论文题目就是"共同基金根本不可能超越市场平均水平"（1951）。1973 年《漫步华尔街》出版，其他许多有影响力的研究也紧随其后。又例如，著名经济学家保罗·A.萨缪尔森 * 1974 年发表论文"投资判定的挑衅"，宣布"超卓的投资业绩未得到证实"。[4] 美国投资顾问查尔斯·D.埃利斯 * 1975 年撰文"输家的游戏"，得出了类似的结论："投资管理业务（投资管理应当是一种职业，但其实不是）建立在一个简单而基本的观念上：专业的理财经理人可以战胜市场。但这个前提似乎是错误的。"[5] 同马尔基尔一样，埃利斯推荐一种指数基金，并认为对投资者来说，最好的结果就是取得市场平均收益，因为"如果无法战胜市场，当然应该考虑跟市场站到同一边"。[6]

　　尽管马尔基尔在《漫步华尔街》中的观点在当时既非原创也非独有，但他对投资领域的重要贡献仍然不可低估。很少有理论家能在投资界产生更大的影响；他的《漫步华尔街》让那些投资观点广受欢迎，改变了投资界，并帮助创立了一种新型的共同基金。《漫步华尔街》引发的关于"战胜市场"的辩论已经持续了40多年。[7]

---

1. 伯顿·G.马尔基尔：《漫步华尔街：股市历久弥新的成功投资策略》，纽约：W. W.诺顿公司，2015 年，第 230 页。

2. 马尔基尔：《漫步华尔街》，第 226—227 页。

3. 尤金·F.法玛："有效资本市场：理论与实证研究回顾"，《金融学报》第 25 卷，1970 年 5 月第 2 期。

4. 保罗·A.萨缪尔森："投资判定的挑衅"，《证券投资管理杂志》第 1 卷，1974 年第 1 期，第 17 页。

5. 查尔斯·D.埃利斯："输家的游戏"，《金融分析师期刊》第 31 卷，1975 年 7/8 月第 4 期，第 19 页。

6. 埃利斯："输家的游戏"，第 26 页。

7. "投资巨星：伯顿·马尔基尔"，傻瓜投资指南网站，登录日期 2015 年 11 月 21 日，http://news.fool.co.uk/news/investing/2011/01/04/investment-greats-burton-malkiel.aspx。

第二部分：学术思想

5 思想主脉

要点 ⚷

- 马尔基尔在《漫步华尔街》中有两个核心主题：有效市场假说，和投注于整个股市而不是个股的"聪明"投资方法。
- 《漫步华尔街》用数据表明，宽基指数基金能反映股票市场的整体价值，其历史业绩优于其他任何股市投资策略。
- 马尔基尔用直截了当、通俗易懂的语言有力地论证了为什么他的投资方法优于投机——简而言之，即押注于短期利润。

核心主题

伯顿·G.马尔基尔的《漫步华尔街：股市历久弥新的成功投资策略》有两个核心主题贯穿全书。第一个是有效市场假说；第二个是"投机"与"投资"的重大区别。

根据随机漫步理论，股价变动完全不可预测。遵循有效市场假说，市场"如此有效——当信息出现时，价格迅速变动——没有人能够通过快速买入或卖出而获利。而且真正的新闻是随机出现的，是不可预测的"。[1]那么投资者的核心问题就来了：如何估计股票的"真实价值"，确保在购入股票时不超额支出，或者如何购买价值被低估的股票，从而"战胜市场"？[2]

正如马尔基尔多次直截了当地指出：这是不可能的。没有投资者能够长期战胜市场，因为"挑选优质股票或预测市场总体走势的机会均等。你的猜中几率和猿猴、股票经纪人甚至和我都一样"。[3]

一旦认清（至少在马尔基尔看来）这一事实，真正的"投资者"便可以运用有效市场假说明智地投资。投资方法很简单，只要购买宽基指数基金（购入大量不同股票并持有的一种基金），投注于市场本身就行了。如此，投资的回报就拟合了整个股市的长期回报，实际上保证了主要收益。只有愚蠢的"投机者"才会继续追求短期的超额回报。由于市场是"随机漫步"，超额回报是不可能持续的——有效市场假说已经清晰说明了这一点，但从事投资业务的人会始终否认（显然出于利己的原因：他们已经承诺为客户赚取高于市场平均水平的收益，要保护自己为客户打理财富而收取的管理费）。

> "反常现象可能会出现，市场可能变得非理性地乐观，而且会经常吸引毫无戒心的投资者。但最终，真正的价值会被市场发现，这是投资者必须注意的主要教训。"
>
> ——伯顿·G.马尔基尔：《漫步华尔街》

思想探究

《漫步华尔街》认为，有效市场假说在真实的股票市场中，包括纽约证券交易所*，都是成立的。若非如此，"战胜市场"要容易得多。但马尔基尔有力地证明了，要战胜市场有多么困难："一名投资者在1969年初投资了10 000美元到标准普尔500指数基金，假设所有红利再投，到2014年6月的市值为736 196美元。另一名投资者同期花同样的本金购买一般的主动式管理基金，到2014年6月，他的投资价值增长到501 470美元。二者的差距之大可见一斑。"[4]

也就是说，投资分散并遵循有效市场假说（只是简单地购买大量不同公司的股票）的指数基金的收益是所谓的"专业"投资经理管理的基金的近 1.5 倍。这个时间跨度包括许多个股票市场的"牛市"和"熊市"，但从长期来看，指数共同基金的表现仍要好得多。这些数字清楚地表明，只要时间足够长，华尔街就能够兑现承诺，并指明了更明智的投资方式。那么，为什么更多的人不把钱投入长期指数共同基金呢？是因为许多人对"投机"比"投资"更感兴趣，《漫步华尔街》里对此作了一个重要区分。

在马尔基尔看来，投资者"买入股票，期望股票在未来几年或几十年的时间里产生可靠的现金回报和资本收益"。[5] 与此相反，投机者"买入股票，期望在接下来的几天或几周内获得一笔短期回报"。[6] 投机行为经常买进处于上升趋势中的股票迅速获利，马尔基尔反对这种行为，将之称为"全民疯狂"。从 17 世纪荷兰郁金香球茎热 * 开始（当时竞争将郁金香球茎的价格炒到天文数字，随后很快出现了价格崩盘），马尔基尔总结了一系列类似的"泡沫"。最终事实证明，这些泡沫对买进的投资者来说都是灾难性的。马尔基尔的观点始终清晰："一段时期最热门的股票或基金总是在下一个时期表现最差。"[7] 迅速致富的共同愿望使得投机者很容易被华尔街承诺"战胜市场"的策略所俘虏。在某种程度上，马尔基尔完全赞同金融诈骗犯查尔斯·庞兹（庞氏骗局的创始人，用新来投资者注入的资金支付向先期投资者承诺的高回报）的说法："当一个人的目光锁定在一件事情上时，就形同盲目。"[8]

马尔基尔接着评论了许多不同形式的主动投资策略（"主动"意为买入和卖出股票的频率比马尔基尔主张的被动方法要频繁得多）。这些主动策略仍然声称能"战胜市场"，其中包括技术分析

（分析过去的价格走势，以期预测未来的趋势）和基本面分析（寻求股票的"真实价值"）。他还研究了试图平衡股票风险的现代投资组合理论，以及新出现的行为金融学。后者研究了投资的心理方面（如"羊群行为"——大众心理的影响）。马尔基尔在这个相对较新的领域得到了一些启发，但他认为启发相当有限。

马尔基尔的结论明确而又始终如一，"投资组合的核心应当包括低成本、节税费、广分散的指数基金"，这样才能保证市场回报。[9]

语言表述

马尔基尔旨在为读者提供一份可读性强的投资和金融指南，其中包括对投资理论与实践的学术进展的探讨。[10] 他将自己的见解融入复杂的投资模型，并配以清晰的阐释。他的写作风格是谈话式、非正式和友好的，有时甚至是幽默的。例如，有一处他写道："如果你的经纪人打电话说将为你提供 IPO（首次公开募股*）股票，可以打赌，新发行的这只股票是个蹩脚货。"[11]——即不是特别有价值。然而，有时他采用一种更为专业的笔触，可能有些让人生厌，甚至觉得他高高在上。例如，他在某个地方写道："认真的读者现在会注意到，在示意图中……"，然后再向读者陈述信息。[12]

马尔基尔的思想之所以有如此强大的影响力，与其说是因为这些思想的独创性，倒不如说是因为他的表达方式。例如当股票价格意外下跌时，重要的是不恐慌和不抛售，这一简单的观点在马尔基尔的描述下变得十分有力："如果投资者坚持买入持有策略，会看到 1900 年投入道琼斯工业平均指数*（在纽约股票交易所交易的 30 只股票平均值）的 1 美元到 2013 年年初将升值为 290 美元。然而，倘若投资者错过了每年最好的 5 个交易日，那么，在 2013 年，这 1 美元的投资价值还不足 1 美分。" [13]

---

1. 伯顿·G.马尔基尔：《漫步华尔街：股市历久弥新的成功投资策略》，纽约：W. W. 诺顿公司，2015 年，第 184 页。
2. 马尔基尔：《漫步华尔街》，第 105 页。
3. 马尔基尔：《漫步华尔街》，第 190 页。
4. 马尔基尔：《漫步华尔街》，第 17 页。
5. 马尔基尔：《漫步华尔街》，第 28 页。
6. 马尔基尔：《漫步华尔街》，第 28 页。
7. 马尔基尔：《漫步华尔街》，第 254 页。
8. 道格拉斯·H.邓恩：《庞兹》，纽约：麦格劳—希尔国际出版公司，1975 年，第 134 页。
9. 马尔基尔：《漫步华尔街》，第 261 页。
10. 马尔基尔：《漫步华尔街》，第 18 页。
11. 马尔基尔：《漫步华尔街》，第 257 页。
12. 马尔基尔：《漫步华尔街》，第 214 页。
13. 马尔基尔：《漫步华尔街》，第 157 页。

6 思想支脉

要点 🔑

- 马尔基尔详细分析了"新派投资技术"——投资理论和策略；但并不相信它们有用。

- 马尔基尔探究了"系统性风险"*，认为分散投资（购买大量不同股票来创造多样化的投资组合）并不能应对增加的风险。

- 对于某些重大问题，马尔基尔并未给出答案，例如万一再次出现导致 2007—2008 年金融崩溃的资产泡沫破裂会怎样：股市本身能否幸存？

其他思想

伯顿·G.马尔基尔的《漫步华尔街：股市历久弥新的成功投资策略》第 11 版对"技术分析"和"基本面分析"一笔带过，转而剖析新的投资方法。他仔细分析了一些新派投资方法。这些方法被他嘲讽地称为"在学术塔中闭门造就的纯粹'新派投资技术'"，但在当今的投资界中仍常受到追捧。[1]

在这些新投资方法中，马尔基尔首先探讨了现代投资组合理论。该理论试图平衡投资组合内部的风险以期产生超额收益。马尔基尔还研究了"资本-资产定价模型"*。该模型主要认为，必须提高投资组合的总体风险水平才能获得较高回报。要正确地做到这一点，需要遵循一种被称为"贝塔"的神秘方法。[2]股票的"贝塔值"反映股票价格对总体市场波动的敏感性。

马尔基尔还评论了行为金融学。行为金融学研究非理性的市场行为，包括判断偏差、羊群心理、过度自信和损失厌恶（避免损失的愿望）等，以便从这些行为造成的股票价格与其实际价值之间的缺口中牟利。尽管马尔基尔发现这个模型有不少缺陷，但他从中获得了许多启发，进一步丰富了自己的"随机漫步"模型。

最后，马尔基尔提供了一份"随机漫步者与其他投资者的实用指南"，展示了如何将他的随机漫步模型运用于个人财务的各个方面。

> "在投资方面，我们往往是自己最大的敌人。"
>
> —— 伯顿·G. 马尔基尔：《漫步华尔街》

思想探究

现代投资组合理论试图将各种风险较高——潜在收益也较高——的股票结合起来，以期达到风险平衡。例如，对海岛经济感兴趣的人可能会同时投资大型海滩度假村和雨伞制造商。这样一来，无论岛上天气如何，他都可以赚钱。[3] 马尔基尔指出，问题在于大多数公司的命运往往朝着相同的方向发展。"当经济衰退造成人们失业时，他们既不去暑期度假也不购买雨伞。因此，在现实中人们不应指望能达到上述的风险抵消效果。"[4]

2007—2009 年的全球经济衰退*等事件便是如此。当时所有市场同时下跌，无论投资如何组合，持有风险最大的股票的人遭受了最惨重的损失。于是马尔基尔评论道："难怪有些投资者开始认为分散投资似乎不再是有效的风险防范策略。"[5]

投资者发明了多种"智能贝塔"策略*（试图捕捉市场低效的

数学公式），力图在不增加风险的情况下实现更高的回报。[6] 马尔基尔质疑这些策略的价值，他写道："尽管涉及数学运算，但贝塔策略背后的基本思想是把一些精确的数字强加在理财经理人多年来的主观感受上。"换言之，复杂的数学实际上是被用来支撑"直觉"或远非客观的一众观点。[7]

马尔基尔发现，这个理论在面临"系统性风险"时——所有股票的走势都与市场整体同步——同样分崩离析了。[8] 在探讨现代投资组合理论时，马尔基尔证明这种系统性风险（即整个市场价值下跌的风险）"并不能通过分散（例如，通过购买多种股票的组合来分散风险）来化解"。他还运用这一逻辑否定了所有试图确定股票核心价值的模型（"资本-资产定价模型"）。股票的核心价值可能与交易价格不同。即使有投资者发现了"定价低效"（即股价未能反映公司的实际价值），其他投资者也会观察到同样的情况，股价也几乎立即被市场纠正：模型会准确找出定价偏低的股票，"投资者则会抓住机会争取更高的回报，从而推高股票价格"。[9]

至于行为金融学，马尔基尔完全不认同非理性行为会导致股价过高或过低的观点。"有效市场理论的追随者相信，聪明、理性的交易者会纠正任何非理性交易者引起的错误定价。"[10] 马尔基尔也承认行为金融学的见解对普通投资者"非常有帮助"。[11] 了解这些干扰性、非理性的动因对于任何投资者来说都是好事（尽管无所不知的市场最终会淘汰一切非理性的干扰动因）。

被忽视之处

马尔基尔的有效市场假说得到了许多学术文献的支持。正如马尔基尔在《漫步华尔街》中反复强调的，资产泡沫（描述股票或其他资产价格超过其实际价值的术语）最终一定会自我修正。投资者会意识到价格不会继续走高，然后大规模抛售。这种突然抛售将导致公司股价暴跌，使其接近股票的实际价值。

然而，马尔基尔从未谈及市场本身是否足够强大，能应对日益加剧的危机。当2007—2008年次贷危机*（一场基于美国风险抵押贷款交易的金融危机）的泡沫破裂时，政府需要提供救助来保护股票市场。随着时间的推移，危机的规模变得越来越大，不再是孤立的灾难，这是一个明显而现实的危险。例如，2007—2008年的全球金融危机可被视为"财政赤字、纳税人救助和华尔街忘恩负义模式的最近一次重演。所有迹象表明，这种模式必定会持续下去"。[12]

如果有一天危机规模过大，政府无法挽救股市崩盘，投资者将失去一切——甚至包括那些把钱投入宽基指数基金的"聪明的"投资者。这种假设并非无稽之谈，但是马尔基尔从未考虑过这种可能性。

---

1. 伯顿·G.马尔基尔：《漫步华尔街：股市历久弥新的成功投资策略》，纽约：W.W.诺顿公司，2015年，第189页。
2. 马尔基尔：《漫步华尔街》，第210页。
3. 马尔基尔：《漫步华尔街》，第197—199页。
4. 马尔基尔：《漫步华尔街》，第199页。
5. 马尔基尔：《漫步华尔街》，第204页。
6. 马尔基尔：《漫步华尔街》，第260—261页。

7. 马尔基尔:《漫步华尔街》, 第 210 页。

8. 马尔基尔:《漫步华尔街》, 第 210 页。

9. 马尔基尔:《漫步华尔街》, 第 215 页。

10. 马尔基尔:《漫步华尔街》, 第 230 页。

11. 马尔基尔:《漫步华尔街》, 第 230 页。

12. 保罗·克鲁格曼和罗宾·韦尔斯:"泡沫破裂规模继续变大:为什么?",《纽约书评》, 2011 年 7 月 14 日, 登录日期 2016 年 2 月 16 日, http://www.nybooks.com/articles/2011/07/14/busts-keep-getting-bigger-why/。

7 历史成就

要点 &

- 在力推有效市场假说的同时，马尔基尔认为投资界的传统观点几乎都是无稽之谈。40 多年来，读者和投资者积极回应他的观点。

- 《漫步华尔街》汇集并进一步发展了 20 世纪 70 年代初的许多投资理论趋势，主要是围绕有效市场假说的投资理论。

- 2007—2008 年的金融崩溃挑战了马尔基尔的方法；批评人士辩称，与房地产市场挂钩的价格泡沫表明市场未能为那些资产找到正确的价格，但马尔基尔表示有效市场假说模型是有效的——几年之后泡沫破裂，价格最终回归到正常水平。

观点评价

《漫步华尔街：股市历久弥新的成功投资策略》的写作意图很明确："关于股市有太多扑朔迷离的说法，需要一本书来正本清源。"[1] 在这里，"正本清源"意味着接受股票市场价格反映该股票当前所有可知信息的观点。股票的历史价格波动模式不能预测未来的走势，且股票在任何特定时间的"真实价值"都是一种估值，从来都不是精确的。只有市场（随着时间的推移）会揭示哪些股票的核心价值在不断增长（反映在股价上涨），哪些没有增长。

这些观点均源自 20 世纪 60 年代末至 70 年代初的投资理论和有效市场假说。从那时起，那些观点便如《漫步华尔街》一书一样经久不衰。《漫步华尔街》2015 年第 11 版的序言反映了马尔基尔的分析经受住了快速变化的世界的考验；1973 年《漫步华尔街》

第 1 版问世时，许多东西都不存在，其中包括金融领域每日习以为常的东西，如自动出纳机、各色现代交易技术、共同基金和免税基金——"金融界的变化不胜枚举"。[2]

然而，在这个充斥着复杂投资策略的新世界里，马尔基尔对有效市场假说仍有把握："如今，四十多年过去了，我更加笃信原来那篇论文。"[3]

这一论断仍然广为流传，也十分可信——并被投资数万亿美元于宽基指数共同基金的投资者奉为真理。这也反映了马尔基尔的杰出成就。

> "与 10 位理财专家交谈，你可能会听到 10 个人都推荐伯顿·马尔基尔的经典投资书籍。"
>
> —— 安德莉亚·库姆斯 *，《华尔街日报》

当时的成就

《漫步华尔街》首次出版于 1973 年，当时华尔街处于一个完全不同的时代：有效市场假说刚刚被实证（基于数据的证据）所证实（见尤金·F. 法玛 1970 年发表的里程碑式的文章"有效资本市场：理论与实证研究回顾"）。[4] 有效市场假说逐渐被投资理论家普遍接受。同样，在现实的投资界中，有效市场假说的影响也越来越大：约翰·博格尔在 1974 年成立了先锋集团，并在不久之后推出了第一只指数共同基金。马尔基尔的《漫步华尔街》是这一进程的核心部分，把这些观点传播给了非专业的"普通"投资者。

在过去 42 年里，马尔基尔定期修改《漫步华尔街》，探讨新的投资理论和实践。同时，越来越多的学者和投资者对马尔基尔的结论提出了异议。于是，那些仍然相信自己能够"主动"管理财富而"战胜市场"的人与像马尔基尔这样信奉长期投资指数共同基金，采取"被动"策略的人展开了一场激烈的讨论。[5] 然而，2007—2008 年的金融崩溃，伴随着住房和股票市场崩盘——这是自 20 世纪 20 年代和 30 年代大萧条 * 以来最严重的危机——可能产生了新证据，在理论和实践上削弱了有效市场假说的可信度。这场辩论仍在继续。

局限性

《漫步华尔街》在投资理论界和实践中依旧享有盛名。但在学者们越来越多的质疑声中，马尔基尔始终坚定捍卫随机漫步模型。2003 年，他写道："到 21 世纪初，有效市场假说的主导地位已经有所动摇。许多金融经济学家和统计学家开始相信我们至少可以部分预测股票价格。"[6]

马尔基尔承认，由于投资者的非理性或错误判断，"随着时间的推移，可能会出现股票价格不正常甚至股票收益可预测的现象，甚至可能短期持续下去"。但他并不认为这种低效会长期持续——持续的时间决不足以让投资者找出获得超额回报的策略。[7]

2007—2008 年的金融崩溃给有效市场假说带来了严峻的考验。在危机出现前的几年，银行和其他金融公司一直在创造和出售各式基于住房抵押贷款的证券。这些投资工具的价格持续上涨，直至崩盘，其中许多失去了大部分或全部价值。然而，在"有效"的市场中，这些资产的价格怎么会被如此大幅高估？许多人认为这次危机说明有效市场假说已经过时，因为"市场失灵了"。[8] 对马尔基尔而言，这种怀疑只不过是对有效市场假说的一种误解。"有效市场假说并不意味着市场总是正确的。"他在 2012 年某次电视访谈中谈到那场金融危机时如是说。[9]"市场往往是错的。关键是没有人知道市场什么时候错了——价格是错误的，但没有人知道价格是太高了还是太低了。市场是不可战胜的，但这并不意味着市场是正确的。"[10]

在马尔基尔看来，市场只有经历过长期修正才会"正确"：2007—2008 年的泡沫破裂后，资产和股票的价格回落到更接近其真实价值的水平。马尔基尔认为，泡沫确会破裂，却恰好再次有力地证明有效市场假说成立。

最后，《漫步华尔街》依靠来自股市的实证数据（实际交易价格的记录，而不是理论）。如果数据不再能证明有效市场假说，那么整本书就不攻自破。到目前为止，有效市场假说从长期来看一直是正确的。然而，有效市场假说在短期或中期，或发生价格剧烈波动时具有较大局限性——像 2007—2008 年的金融崩溃，可能会威胁到整个金融体系。

1. 伯顿·G.马尔基尔：《漫步华尔街：股市历久弥新的成功投资策略》，纽约：W.W.诺顿公司，2015 年，第 18 页。
2. 马尔基尔：《漫步华尔街》，第 18 页。
3. 马尔基尔：《漫步华尔街》，第 17 页。
4. 拉米·马侯治，"金融市场环境"，开放大学，登录日期 2016 年 2 月 16 日，http://www.open.edu/openlearn/money-management/money/accounting-and-finance/the-financial-markets-context/content-section—acknowledgements。

5. 马尔基尔：《漫步华尔街》，第254页。

6. 伯顿·G.马尔基尔："有效市场假说及其批评"，《经济展望杂志》第17卷，2003年第1期，第60页。

7. 马尔基尔："有效市场假说及其批评"，第80页。

8. 山姆·罗："金融奇才伯顿·马尔基尔捍卫有效市场假说"，登录日期2015年11月25日，http://www.businessinsider.com/burton-malkiel-efficient-market-hypothesis-2012-4?IR=T。

9. 罗："金融奇才伯顿·马尔基尔"。

10. 罗："金融奇才伯顿·马尔基尔"。

8 著作地位

要点

- 马尔基尔毕生致力于关注有效市场假说或称作随机漫步理论，以及如何将其运用于现实的股票市场。

- 马尔基尔认为，"封闭式基金"*，即通过发行固定数量的份额一次性筹集资本的基金，是唯一一种可能获得较高投资回报的主动交易型基金。

- 尽管马尔基尔也有许多关于投资理论和实践的其他方面的著作，但迄今为止，《漫步华尔街》仍然是最为知名、被研究最多的一部。

定位

1973 年《漫步华尔街：股市历久弥新的成功投资策略》出版时，伯顿·G. 马尔基尔已经是美国顶尖的学者，任普林斯顿大学经济学教授。他当时已出版了有关国际货币政策、利率结构和证券期权等多部著作，发表了大量有影响力的文章。然而，《漫步华尔街》成了他职业生涯的至高点，很快成为全国畅销书。如今这本书仍然是学术界和专业金融服务界关注和争议最多的著作之一。

《漫步华尔街》也是一项持续的成就：这本书已经发行了 11 版，每一版都与之前的版本有很大不同。每个新版本都直接回应了质疑有效市场假说的最新理论，以及当时金融界时新的、更实际的挑战。因此，每个版本的核心基本不变，包括其理论结论——有效市场假说始终成立——以及其投资建议——引导读者转向宽基指数共同基金，都不曾改变。虽然 2007—2008 年的金融崩溃和全球经济衰退让许多投资策略名誉扫地，但马尔基尔在《漫步华尔街》中主张的方法却得到了巩固：投资者只能着眼长远才能免于这类冲击。

> "在创作这本书的 11 个版本中，对我来说最有价值的是我收到了许多投资者的来信，表达了感谢之情。他们告诉我，他们从四十年来一直不变的简单忠告中获益匪浅。那些经久不衰的教诲包括广泛分散、年度再平衡、运用指数基金、并坚持到底。"
>
> ——伯顿·G.马尔基尔：《漫步华尔街》

整合

马尔基尔的职业生涯多姿多彩，他既是学者，又是专业的投资顾问。自 1973 年以来，他不仅出版了 10 余版《漫步华尔街》，还出版了大量关于投资各方面的书籍和文章，譬如：受赠机构应当如何管理风险（受赠机构通常指拥有一笔捐款或赠款的学校或其他非营利性机构。一般来说，只能支出赠款的利息）；投资者如何战胜通货膨胀；以及股票价格的结构等。

马尔基尔在《漫步华尔街》中传达的主要信息是，最佳的投资策略通常是将钱投入指数共同基金——吸纳众多投资者的资金，用于购买大量不同公司的股票并长期持有的基金，获取类似于整体股票市场的长期价值增值。这种买入并持有或"被动"的投资方式也比频繁买卖寻求短期利润的"主动"共同基金的管理费率更低。

虽然马尔基尔通常不赞同主动投资，但有一种类型例外："封闭式基金"。[1] 这种观点出现在他 1977 年发表的一篇颇具影响力的文章"封闭式投资公司股票的估值"中。文章也探析了这种独特基金所带来的机会。

封闭式基金与共同基金一样，都是主动管理型基金，但结构完全不同。封闭式基金的结构很吸引马尔基尔，尽管这背离了他一贯倡导的被动基金策略。虽然大多数共同基金可以不断接收投资者，但封闭式基金在一开始发行的份额是固定的，一次性筹集资本。这就像是一家公司的首次公开募股，首次向公众发行股票。只是封闭式基金的份额并不像股票那样代表对公司的所有权，而是参与"封闭式基金"的凭证。最为重要的是，封闭式基金份额的价格不仅反映了基金拥有和管理的资产，而且也反映了当时有多少投资者想要购买该基金的份额。[2]

有时，封闭式基金份额的需求量低于基金资产的市场价值。在这种情况下，基金份额的价格可能低于其应有的价值。对于以这种价格买进的人来说，较低的价格代表了一个实际的折扣。如果以这种折扣价买入这只基金的份额，且基金资产与市场的整体表现相匹配，则投资者实际上能获得超额收益，因为投资者是在低位买入。[3]马尔基尔在 2015 版的《漫步华尔街》中仍然同意这种分析，说明该结论仍站得住脚。

可以说，马尔基尔发表的所有著作，哪怕颇具影响的"封闭式投资公司股票的估值"，在《漫步华尔街》的巨大成就前都黯然失色。由于马尔基尔其他的许多著作也对随机漫步理论加以评论和分析，他的全部著作可以说是高度连贯和统一的。

意义

虽然马尔基尔在出版《漫步华尔街》时已经是一位具有高度影响力的学者和成功的投资者，但可以不失公允地说，《漫步华尔街》

是他最好、最重要的著作。尽管有效市场假说是由诺贝尔经济学奖得主尤金·F.法玛定义并用实证数据证明的，但马尔基尔的《漫步华尔街》是长期投资宽基指数共同基金公认的理论依据。指数共同基金现已发展成万亿美元级的业务。《漫步华尔街》在投资理论和实践中的影响不言而喻。马尔基尔也因此受到顶尖学者以及诸如美国人乔治·索罗斯和沃伦·巴菲特*等著名亿万富翁投资者的褒扬或诟病。[4]《漫步华尔街》已被引用了无数次。

尽管马尔基尔著作颇丰，但是《漫步华尔街》奠定了他的声誉。马尔基尔论述过的其他一些主题，例如他专注研究的封闭式基金的折扣，虽然在他的理论和投资观上很有分量，但在公众心目中，不过是他随机漫步模型的一个小小注脚。随机漫步理论提出了股票领域最大的问题：能否预测市场走势从而稳定地赚取超额投资回报？整个金融界总是说，也必须经常说，只要你够聪明的话，绝对可以做到。马尔基尔却传递了战胜市场是不可能的这一观点，并广受欢迎。由于他有大量缜密的证据来支持这个立场，并且能够以平白的语言来表述观点，马尔基尔自然而然地成为那些想抨击随机漫步理论，证明股票价格可以预测的专家和竞争对手们的攻击目标。

尤为重要的是，马尔基尔称《漫步华尔街》所涉及的读者主要是经常被华尔街的专业人士所蒙骗的"普通投资者"。那些华尔街的专业人士声称自己拥有的洞察力实际上是不存在的。

1. 伯顿·G.马尔基尔：《漫步华尔街：股市历久弥新的成功投资策略》，纽约：W.W.诺顿公司，2015年，第401页。
2. 伯顿·G.马尔基尔："封闭式投资公司股票的估值"，《金融学报》第32卷，1977年6月第3期，第847页。
3. 马尔基尔："封闭式投资公司股票的估值"，第858页。
4. 更多例子参见乔治·索罗斯："索罗斯：金融市场"，《金融时报》，2009年10月17日，登录日期2016年2月19日，http://www.ft.com/intl/cms/s/2/dbc0e0c6-bfe9-11de-aed2-00144feab49a.html#axzz40d8gJIsO；沃伦·巴菲特："超级投资者格雷厄姆和多德斯维尔"，哥伦比亚大学商学院杂志《Hermes》，1984年5月17日。

第三部分：学术影响

9 最初反响

要点 🔑

- 虽然批评人士称股票市场中的确存在价格低效，可以用来获利（即有可能预测和利用市场中的价格波动），但马尔基尔认为，长期来看，这种低效现象会消失，因而有效市场假说的方法仍然更好。

- 世界上最著名的投资者沃伦·巴菲特坚持认为，市场上可以利用的低效现象有很多；他本人成功的投资记录便是铁证。

- 马尔基尔承认价格泡沫已经存在了几个世纪，但他辩称，这显然是非理性和低效的市场行为，但从长远来看，泡沫终将破裂，市场仍旧有效。

批评

对于伯顿·G.马尔基尔的《漫步华尔街：股市历久弥新的成功投资策略》的评论大部分是正面的，不断有研究表明股票市场确实是有效的。[1]"有效"在这里意指市场会为每一只股票找到合适的价格，准确地反映股票所代表的公司的所有已知信息；如果公开的信息表明一个公司业绩良好或差强人意，投资者就会把公司股票的价格抬高或压低。然而，自20世纪70年代以来，有效市场假说的权威地位受到越来越多的挑战，许多金融经济学家和统计学家开始相信股票价格至少部分是可预测的。[2]

其中一项主要的批评研究是由来自麻省理工学院和宾夕法尼亚大学的商学研究者联袂打造的，名为（略带讽刺意味的）《华尔街的非随机漫步》（1999）。该研究从数学的角度证明股票市场中的确存在低效现象，可以被主动投资者利用，以此反驳马尔基尔的观点。[3] 在《漫步华尔街》第 11 版中，马尔基尔很乐意承认这一点："股票市场与数学家的理想不完全一致。理想的状态是当前价格走势完全独立于过去的价格。"[4] 但他的回应是，那又怎样？"存在的系统性关联通常很小，对投资者没有帮助，"他这样写道，系统性关联敌不过频繁交易而产生的费用和资本利得税。[5] 换言之，有时候过去表现强劲的某公司的股票价格会继续上涨，而非下跌，仅仅是因投资者的预期而起。然而，这种"可预测"的价格变动幅度可能很小，如果把钱交给投资专业人士，试图利用这种价格变化，专业人士收取的费用往往会抵消他们能为客户创造的一切收益。

其他批评者认为，投资者经历了过于乐观和过度悲观的浪潮，导致股价明显偏离（进一步上升或下跌）。[6] 还有一些批评人士发现了"季节性或周内效应模式"；例如，一月份的交易似乎具有一定的规律。[7] 诚然，尤金·F. 法玛在 1993 年的一项研究中注意到，在很长一段时间内，小公司的股票往往比大公司的股票收益率更高。[8]

现实世界的投资者一直是最激烈的批评者，其中最著名的是投资者沃伦·巴菲特，他公然抨击了有效市场假说。巴菲特称，优秀的投资者会寻找"企业的价值与企业在股市上的价格之间的缺口"——也就是所谓的基本面分析法。[9]

> "我深信市场上有很多低效现象。"
>
> ——沃伦·巴菲特

回应

马尔基尔一一回应了对自己理论的各种质疑。例如，2003 年，他在"有效市场假说及其批评"一文中总结了他对所有主要批评的回应。在列举了各种批评意见，并分析各自的论点之后，马尔基尔用实证来检验那些投资策略。他称实证表明："这些（他们所设想的成功投资的）模式在不同的采样时期内并不坚实可靠。"[10] 此外，他补充道："这些模式中有许多即使确实存在，将来也会自我毁灭，已经有许多不攻自破了。"[11]

换言之，市场反常的消息一经传出，反常的市场现象即刻就消失了。在某种程度上，这也支持了有效市场假说，因为一旦市场优势变得众所周知，很快就会成为常态。最终，马尔基尔得出结论是："我们的股票市场远比最近的一些学术论文所想的更有效、更不可预测。"——如今他还继续坚持这个立场。[12]

对于像沃伦·巴菲特这样年复一年"击败市场"的卓越投资者，马尔基尔持谨慎的态度。《漫步华尔街》的第 11 版暗示沃伦·巴菲特的成功纯粹是靠运气："我愈发深信，共同基金经理的过往记录在预测未来成功方面毫无价值。持续表现卓越的少数几个例子出现的几率也就跟碰运气不相上下。"[13] 这个观点也十分公允：随机漫步必然会产生少数长期赢家。

冲突与共识

虽然人们对《漫步华尔街》的看法总体是正面的，但经济学家查尔斯·P.金德尔伯格和罗伯特·Z.阿利伯认为有效市场假说本质上建立在一个理性信念的前提下，即"投资者对经济变量的变化做出反应，仿佛他们总能完全意识到这些变化的长期影响"——但这是不可能的。[14] 有效市场假说这种"理性行为"的假设一直受到金德尔伯格、罗伯特·J.希勒和行为经济学领域其他人的猛烈抨击。

诸如《华尔街的非随机漫步》等专著用实证表明股票价格是可预测的，因此有效市场假说显然并非滴水不漏。

但是马尔基尔从不认为存在完全可靠的有效市场假说。《漫步华尔街》清楚地描述了过去巨大的非理性泡沫——从17世纪荷兰的郁金香球茎热到21世纪的次贷危机。虽然这不是有效的市场行为，但没有人可以永远准确地把握市场何时达到顶峰，甚至最聪明的投资者有时也会抓住资产太久不放（在价格大幅跳水之后），因而从长远来看证实了有效市场假说。诚如马尔基尔所言："股市在短期内是投票机，长期是称重秤。股票真正的价值最终会体现出来。在真相出来之前，投资者无法稳定利用任何可能存在的异常情况或投资模式。"

马尔基尔十分谨慎，主张有效市场假说的成立条件是从长期来看的——然而他的批评者有时似乎会忽视这一点。同样，他认为，只有当人们能够预测谁能成为战胜市场的成功投资者，而不是事后评论，沃伦·巴菲特的长期突出业绩才会威胁到有效市场假说。[15]"将来还会有沃伦·巴菲特出现，"马尔基尔承认，"可能有几个沃伦·巴菲特，但问题是：我不知道谁会是下一个沃伦·巴菲特，我认为其他人也不知道；寻找下一个沃伦·巴菲特就像是大海捞针一样。"[16]

---

1. 乔纳森·克拉克等："有效市场假说"，罗伯特·C.阿尔法编，《专家财务规划：行业领导者的投资策略》，纽约：约翰威立出版社，2001年，第132页。

2. 伯顿·G.马尔基尔："有效市场假说及其批评"，《经济展望杂志》第17卷，2003年第1期，第60页。

3. 罗闻全和A.克雷格·麦金勒：《华尔街的非随机漫步》，普林斯顿；牛津：普林斯顿大学出版社，1999年，第4页。

4. 伯顿·G.马尔基尔：《漫步华尔街：股市历久弥新的成功投资策略》，纽约：W.W.诺顿公司，2015年，第139页。

5. 马尔基尔：《漫步华尔街》，第140页。

6. 沃纳·F.M.德邦特和理查德·塞勒："股市是否反应过度？"，《金融学报》第40卷，1985年7月，第793页。

7. 罗伯特·A.豪根和约瑟夫·拉科尼肖克：《令人难以置信的一月效应：股市未解之谜》，霍姆德：道琼斯-欧文出版社，1987年。

8. 马尔基尔："有效市场假说及其批评"，第67—68页。

9. 沃伦·巴菲特："超级投资者格雷厄姆和多德斯维尔"，哥伦比亚大学商学院杂志《Hermes》，1984年5月17日，第7页。

10. 马尔基尔："有效市场假说及其批评"，第71页。

11. 马尔基尔："有效市场假说及其批评"，第71页。

12. 马尔基尔："有效市场假说及其批评"，第60页。

13. 马尔基尔：《漫步华尔街》，第398页。

14. 罗伯特·Z.阿利伯和查尔斯·P.金德尔伯格：《疯狂、惊恐和崩溃：金融危机史》，伦敦：帕尔格雷夫·麦克米伦出版社，2015年，第53页。

15. 克拉克："有效市场假说"，第131页。

16. 麦克·格里尔："战胜市场就像相信圣诞老人"，傻瓜投资指南网站，登录日期2014年11月25日，http://www.fool.com/investing/general/2010/09/16/beating-the-market-is-like-believing-in-santa.aspx。

10 后续争议

要点 &—

- 虽然马尔基尔认为股票市场总会找到"正确"价格的理论已经非常流行，但（至少在短期内）要知道投资者是否会对影响公司股价的公开新闻反应过度或反应不足并不容易。

- 新的研究依旧表明，模拟猴子投掷飞镖挑出的股票的收益至少与许多专人管理的投资基金相当。

- 马尔基尔对有效市场假说的理论支持广为流传，有着深远的影响；尽管《漫步华尔街》仍然存在争议，但该书在关于股票市场如何运作的持续争论中占据着核心地位。

应用与问题

伯顿·G. 马尔基尔的《漫步华尔街：股市历久弥新的成功投资策略》处于投资理论和实践革新的前沿——认为可以忽略个人投资者的智力和专长，投注于市场本身。其中的关键在于对有效市场假说的审慎定义，即股票价格反映了当时有关公司所有的已知信息。

有效市场假说面临的一大挑战是：投资者对公开信息的反应会有很大的差异，"公众"可能对相关新闻反应过度或反应不足。当出现这种情况时，即使股票价格纯粹是由新闻所驱动的，股价也不是总以正确的方式受到影响。这就使得市场价格波动问题归入了市场非理性行为的范畴中。市场非理性行为继续质疑有效市场假说。例如，某只复杂的对冲基金*（用高风险方法管理的大量不同投资者筹集的资金池）可能会趁股票价格上升的泡沫出现时买入，以便

"乘势"而上，然后（希望）及时退出。这无异于直接打了马尔基尔的脸。马尔基尔声称"聪明的理性交易者会纠正一切因非理性交易者而产生的定价错误"。[1] 换言之，马尔基尔认为，聪明的投资者会抛售任何看似出现价格泡沫的股票，因为泡沫随时都可能破裂，让投资者遭殃。然而，有时投资者的行为会由于非理性的原因，比如贪婪，而背道而驰。

> "支持这个（随机漫步）理论的文献十分丰富，其中不乏最高质量的著作。因此，无论我们终究是否同意这一理论，我们至少必须认真对待它。"
>
> ——罗伯特·J. 希勒：《非理性繁荣》

思想流派

40多年来，《漫步华尔街》仍是被援引最多的投资书籍之一。不断有大量证券分析师、学者和其他投资者受到了该书的影响，或因为推崇其他的投资方法而不得不对抗该书。

《漫步华尔街》并未独创一门学派，而是反映了一种思潮：大量学者和投资者如潮水般涌来，开始质疑共同基金经理的业绩，尤其在考虑到基金经理通常收取的高额费用之后更甚。提到有效市场假说，马尔基尔在《漫步华尔街》中有个著名论断：蒙上眼睛的猴子朝报纸的财经版面投掷飞镖，都能挑出堪比"专家"挑选的股票。[2] 《漫步华尔街》可以被视为对共同基金经理的挑衅："猴子都可以比你们做得更好。"[3]

这个猴子的比喻现在已经发展成型。2014年，知名财经杂志《经济学人》介绍了几项受《漫步华尔街》启发的重要研究。[4] 两个研究团队，一个在加利福尼亚，另一个在伦敦商学院，分别测试比较了基金经理的业绩与模拟猴子在金融版面投掷飞镖的结果。[5] 他们得出的结论是马尔基尔太过谦虚了："模拟猴子投掷飞镖选取的投资组合不仅会击败很多投资者，而且也会跑赢市场。"[6]

当代研究

最近的这些"猴子"研究正反映了《漫步华尔街》仍然处于股票市场如何运作的争议中心，也说明最基本的辩论并没有取得太大的进展。"被动"指数共同基金包含了大量的股票组合，拟合股市的总体回报。长期来看，"被动"指数共同基金会继续跑赢更为"主动"管理的共同基金——尤其是考虑到高昂的管理费用、交易手续费和资本利得税时，更是如此。

尽管如此，依然有人围绕着有效市场假说做了大量学术工作，其中包括与其他投资策略相比，有效市场假说表现如何这个基本问题。最近的《公司财务原理》和《金融市场与金融机构》等著作表明学界在持续探讨市场效率（按照有效市场假说的理想）究竟是什么。[7] 有效市场假说在当今的投资和金融理论界中究竟有多重要，是另一个争论的焦点。罗伯特·J. 希勒凭借其关于市场中非理性行为的研究获得了 2013 年度诺贝尔经济学奖，然而尴尬的是，他最终与有效市场假说之父尤金·F. 法玛共同获得了当年的这一殊荣。后来，希勒公然重申了他的观点，认为有效市场假说只有"一半正确"。[8]

但直至最近，大量基于数据的研究继续证明有效市场假说应用于单个企业的回报和相关指数（即公司列表）时仍然成立。[9] 尽管如此，争论仍然很复杂：虽然所谓的技术分析法在学术界不受待见

（学者们认为技术分析无利可图），但专业投资者依然广泛应用此方法。有人指出，在学术研究中，技术分析法的应用未尽其善。[10] 或者，如同马尔基尔在《漫步华尔街》中多次辩称的，这可能是投资界一种常见的错觉，理财经理人自欺欺人地相信技术分析法是有效的。

经济学家纳西姆·尼古拉斯·塔勒布及其畅销书《黑天鹅：如何应对不可预知的未来》（2007）可以被视为马尔基尔的主要继承者之一。塔勒布认为，对成功的理财经理来说，除却自身能力以外，随机性不仅是股票市场的决定因素，也是更普遍的决定因素。他声称，正是极度不可知、影响深远的事件塑造了我们所知的世界，但我们对此的反应是假装这种随机性不存在。[11] 他继续分析了更广泛的、人类心理上的需求：人类认为未来与过去相似。他指出，这种认知可以为投资者提供真正的金融优势，保护自己免受诸如2007—2008年股市崩盘等恶性市场事件的破坏。塔勒布认为，无视不确定性的严重后果而产生的"系统脆弱性"造成了这次崩盘。[12]

1. 伯顿·G.马尔基尔：《漫步华尔街：股市历久弥新的成功投资策略》，纽约：W.W.诺顿公司，2015年，第230页。

2. 马尔基尔：《漫步华尔街》，第26页。

3. 马尔基尔：《漫步华尔街》，第19页。

4. S. H.："别胡闹了？"，《经济学人》，2014年6月4日，登录日期2015年11月27日，http://www.economist.com/blogs/freeexchange/2014/06/financial-knowledge-and-

investment-performance。

5. 罗伯特·D.阿诺特等："马尔基尔的猴子中令人惊讶的阿尔法和颠倒策略",《投资组合管理期刊》第 39 卷,2013 年夏,第 4 期;安德鲁·克莱尔等："另类股票指数的评估,第 1 部分",伦敦城市大学卡斯商学院,2013 年 3 月,登录日期 2016 年 1 月 10 日,http://www.cassknowledge.com/sites/default/files/article-attachments/evaluation-alternative-equity-indices-part-1-cass-knowledge.pdf。

6. S. H.："别胡闹了？"

7. F. 艾伦等:《公司财务原理》,纽约:麦格劳-希尔／欧文出版社,2011 年,第 314—320 页;G. 埃金斯和 S. 米什金:《金融市场与金融机构》,波士顿:普林帝斯霍尔国际出版有限公司,2012 年,第 117—130 页。

8. 罗伯特·J.希勒："分享诺贝尔荣誉,容忍分歧",《纽约时报》,登录日期 2016 年 1 月 12 日,http://www.nytimes.com/2013/10/27/business/sharing-nobel-honors-and-agreeing-to-disagree.html?hp&_r=0。

9. R. W. 帕克斯和 E. 齐沃特："金融市场效率及其影响",《华盛顿大学投资、资本和金融》,登录日期 2016 年 1 月 12 日,http://faculty.washington.edu/ezivot/econ422/Market%20Efficiency%20EZ.pdf。

10. 奥古斯塔·德古提斯和莉娜·诺维基："有效市场假说:文献与方法论的批判性综述",《经济》第 93 卷,2014 年第 2 期,第 12 页。

11. 纳西姆·尼古拉斯·塔勒布:《黑天鹅:如何应对不可预知的未来》,伦敦:企鹅出版社,2007 年,第 xxii 页。

12. 塔勒布:《黑天鹅》,第 321 页。

11 当代印迹

要点

- 自《漫步华尔街》第 1 版于 1973 年问世的几十年来，投资已经发生了很大的变化，涌现了许多新理论和复杂的数学方法。但是马尔基尔认为，在长期投资中，金融专业人士的表现仍然不敌"蒙住眼睛的猴子"。

- 虽然新的模型试图利用小型股票的价格低效来获利，但一旦考虑到基金经理收取的费用，主动管理基金的收益并不会高于（被动）指数基金。

- 许多学者和投资者仍然决心证明市场上**存在**低效现象，可以持续被"专家"所利用，从而证伪有效市场假说。

地位

伯顿·G.马尔基尔的《漫步华尔街：股市历久弥新的成功投资策略》第 1 版问世已时隔四十余年，对于那些对股票市场如何运作感兴趣的人，或者想要投资股票的人来说，这本书仍然是一本重要的读物。人们对《漫步华尔街》持续不减的热情表明，即便质疑者前仆后继地不断挑战其基本结论，但该书仍然十分重要，且富有说服力。

几十年间，经济发生了巨大的变化。金融服务业在美国爆发式增长，涌现了一系列新的复杂策略，无不承诺"战胜市场"（即产生的收益超出股票市场的平均收益）。这些形形色色的方法必须面对有效市场假说，尤其是马尔基尔的《漫步华尔街》。在《漫步华尔街》第 1 版出版之前，人们想当然地认为华尔街的基金经理能够比猴子更好地投资。但是书出版后，专业人士的投资能力受到严重挑战——威胁到他们在投资过程中的丰厚收入。

在过去的 40 年中，统计分析也发生了变革，其结果是人们能通过算法（一组解决数学问题的规则）和其他数学工具来预测行为。这些发展自然已被应用在股市上赚钱。因此，试图通过数学方程式来预测市场走势的定量分析师＊（或称为"宽客"）变得举足轻重。理财经理人运用这些新的分析方法试图证明股票市场是可预测的，因而对《漫步华尔街》和有效市场假说发出了直接挑战。

> "一场激烈的战斗正在进行。战士们视死如归，因为事关学者的任期和金融专业人士的奖金。这就是为什么我认为大家会喜欢华尔街这种随机漫步的原因。它具备了荡气回肠的戏剧的所有成分——包括财富的得失及其缘由的经典论证。"
>
> ——伯顿·G. 马尔基尔：《漫步华尔街》

互动

可以说，许多信奉"主动"管理方法（相信通过战略买入和卖出股票可以战胜市场）的投资经理人和学术理论家显然致力于证伪有效市场假说。在学术上推翻这一假说对华尔街来说十分有价值，能恢复部分公众对共同基金经理智慧的信任（表明共同基金经理至少比猴子要强）。

在过去几十年里，不断有新的、复杂的学术著作涌现，声称市场上的确存在可利用的低效现象——例如一些难以察觉的"趋势"可以用来预测价格变动。在《漫步华尔街》的第 11 版中，马尔基尔很乐意承认这一点："股票市场与数学家的理想不完全一致。理想的状态是当前价格走势完全独立于过去的价格。"[1] 但是，他也认为"存在的系统性关联通常很小，对投资者没有帮助"。[2]

在投资界，很少有投资者采用的策略能长期战胜市场。在《漫步华尔街》第 11 版中，马尔基尔表示自己甚至愈发怀疑精英投资经理："在本书的前几版中，我提供了几位享有投资组合管理长胜记录的投资经理人名录，并配以简略传记，解释他们的投资风格……在这一版我已经放弃了那种做法。"[3] 马尔基尔越来越相信投资经理人的成功仅仅是缘于运气。[4]

持续争议

在过去的 40 年里，围绕马尔基尔和随机漫步理论的争论没有取得显著进展，马尔基尔对其挑战者的回应也没有多大改变。基金经理之间的竞争十分激烈，争相报出接近股票真实价值的价格，因而几乎没人可以长期超越市场平均水平。新闻影响很快被计入股价。同时，"被动"基金的长期业绩总体良好，仍然优于"主动"基金的表现，而且先进的公式已经证明，市场中的低效现象基本上是微不足道的——产生的收益不会高过股票市场的平均收益。同理，先进的行为金融学也一样：在马尔基尔看来，除非行为金融学的见解能够转化为投资者的长期超额回报，否则不能证明行为金融学优于有效市场假说。

行为金融学虽然影响深远，发展迅速——马尔基尔最新版的《漫步华尔街》还赞扬了行为金融学的洞见和前景——但最终的问题是要长期获得较高的回报。这种关注真实投资者的务实做法是《漫步华尔街》经久不衰的另一大原因。正如某位评论家所说："严格来说，有效市场假说是错的，但它的想法却是极为正确的。"⁵换言之，在短期内，总会出现泡沫、胡乱定价的股票和各种非理性的投资者行为，这看似会动摇有效市场假说。然而，从长期来看，实证数据证实了泡沫终将破裂，价格终将调整到（合理的）准确水平的观点。长期投资者可以指望从中赚钱。

1. 伯顿·G. 马尔基尔：《漫步华尔街：股市历久弥新的成功投资策略》，纽约：W. W. 诺顿公司，2015 年，第 139 页。
2. 马尔基尔：《漫步华尔街》，第 140 页。
3. 马尔基尔：《漫步华尔街》，第 398 页。
4. 马尔基尔：《漫步华尔街》，第 398 页。
5. 马丁·斯威尔："有效市场假说的历史"，《伦敦大学学院研究纪要》第 11 卷，2011 年第 4 期，第 1 页。

12 未来展望

要点 🔑

- 虽然《漫步华尔街》很可能继续保持其影响力,但2007—2008年的金融崩溃几乎让每种经济信仰都深陷泥潭,也可能动摇《漫步华尔街》的公信力。

- 即便股市本身已然进入一个全新、不可预测的时代,但关于股票市场价格波动的讨论始终绕不开《漫步华尔街》。

- 时隔四十余年,《漫步华尔街》依然是投资理论和实践领域援引最广、讨论最多的文献之一。该书依然有很大的影响力,向"主动"共同基金经理发起了强有力的挑战。

潜力

伯顿·G.马尔基尔的《漫步华尔街:股市历久弥新的成功投资策略》在未来数年很可能是备受关注、广受欢迎的股市书籍。顶尖投资者和学者必将不断评论这部著作及其推崇的有效市场假说。大量投资新手必将反复阅读该书,吸收其清晰易懂的信息。

然而,全世界大部分股市的状态(以及全球经济增长总体放缓)让马尔基尔在《漫步华尔街》第11版的结尾变得谨慎起来。他将2000年之后的后互联网泡沫时代称为"祛魅时代","投资者再次领悟到,世道险恶"。[1]虽然投资者在之前的五年中,尤其是在美国股票市场上赚取了丰厚回报,但这在很大程度上是得益于"量化宽松"*政策(印制大量钞票,注入经济,抬高大多数资产的价格,尤其是股票价格)。

让人感到奇怪的是，马尔基尔从未探讨过，联邦政府如此大手笔的干预会怎样改变股票市场的基本动态，或许能让价格上涨变得更可预测。马尔基尔预测"未来一段时间内，我们可能处于低回报期"，[2] 但却不去探究美国天翻地覆的次贷危机会怎样深刻地改变股市的运作方式。暗示股市将会像 1945—2008 年那样运行可能是个有风险的揣测。

> "不要期望股市投资者在 2009—2014 年间获得丰厚回报的情况在未来数年会持续下去。"
>
> —— 伯顿·G. 马尔基尔：《漫步华尔街》

未来方向

《漫步华尔街》的核心信息是投资界竞争过于激烈，没人有长期的内部优势；因而股票价格的变动是完全不可预测的。即使没有更多研究帮衬，这个理论在将来仍然可能具有相当影响力。来自行为金融学等领域的新挑战还将继续出现。但是除非这些竞争学派揭示了一种"战胜市场"的可靠方式，否则不太可能动摇有效市场假说和马尔基尔的《漫步华尔街》的重要地位。

但是，《漫步华尔街》的确把价格泡沫看成是短期的定价错误，只是长期会得到纠正：市场本身会刺破泡沫，导致价格暴跌。这或许是对的，但需要像行为金融学这样的专门知识来揭示资产泡沫如何失控，正如美国次贷危机期间所发生的那样。当时的美联储 *（美国央行）主席艾伦·格林斯潘 * 在股市崩盘前后都坚持认为，股票市场和房地产市场的资产泡沫都应任由其"自爆"。[3] 这么做，格林斯潘——同马尔基尔以及几乎所有其他经济学家一样——也未看清建立在 21 世纪初房地产泡沫之上的巨大金融结构。当泡沫最终自爆时，一连串的连锁反应几乎摧毁了整个经济。

因此，我们需要大量新理论和分析来确保这种情况不会再次发生。虽然随机漫步理论在正常情况下对于理解股票价格可能是有效的，但它并不能保护市场免受这类灾难的冲击。

小结

《漫步华尔街》继续教育人们认清（或反对）声称掌握股票市场优势信息的投资经理人。该书以令人信服的方式拆穿了投资经理人的承诺，用统计数据检验各种盛行的"战胜市场"的策略，并进一步通过有效市场假说直截了当、不加粉饰的逻辑粉碎那些承诺。对于任何打算研究投资或打算投资股票市场的人来说，《漫步华尔街》仍然是必读的。

除了将有效市场假说的主要内容通俗易懂地表达出来，驳斥有人可以经常"战胜市场"的观点外，马尔基尔也为投资者指明了方向。他推荐人们购买并持有宽基指数共同基金，这仍然是中肯的建议——人们也正在采纳其建议。诚如他在《漫步华尔街》第 11 版中所言："2014 年，个人和机构投资者约三分之一的资金投向了指数基金。而且这一比例还在上升。"[4] 尽管 2007—2008 年的金融崩溃造成了系统性危机，但马尔基尔依然坚信，自己的策略经得起时间的考验，在不确定的未来依然能满足投资者的需求："只要大家谨记本书的简单规则和永恒的教训，哪怕在最艰难的时期，也可能安然度过。"[5]

1. 伯顿·G. 马尔基尔：《漫步华尔街：股市历久弥新的成功投资策略》，纽约：W. W. 诺顿公司，2015 年，第 344 页。

2. 马尔基尔：《漫步华尔街》，第 348 页。

3. 关于格林斯潘在金融危机发生前后的观点，请参阅艾伦·格林斯潘："格林斯潘的泡泡浴"，《经济学人》，2002 年 9 月 5 日，登录日期 2016 年 2 月 19 日，http://www.economist.com/node/1314051；"艾伦·格林斯潘：美联储无法阻止市场泡沫"，美国 News Max 财经，2014 年 7 月 24 日，登录日期 2016 年 2 月 19 日，http://www.newsmax.com/Finance/StreetTalk/alan-greenspan-federal-reserve-bubbles-economy/2014/07/24/id/584744/。

4. 马尔基尔：《漫步华尔街》，第 181 页。

5. 马尔基尔：《漫步华尔街》，第 411 页。

术语表

1. **美国金融协会**：《金融学报》的出版机构，是一个以金融经济学为基础的组织（其宗旨是促进金融经济学知识的发展）。

2. **行为金融学**：探索金融市场参与者心理特征的一个金融研究领域，力图揭示市场走势，尤其是反复出现的非理性错误。

3. **泡沫**：一种显著的资产过度定价。

4. **资本-资产定价模型**：认为必须提高投资组合的总体风险水平才能获得超额回报的模型。

5. **资本利得税**：投资者在卖出股票时必须为股票（资本）升值的部分支付的增值税。

6. **封闭式基金**：通过发行固定数量的份额一次性募集资金的基金；封闭式基金份额的价格不仅反映基金所拥有和管理的资产规模，而且也反映发行当时有多少投资者想要购买该基金的份额。

7. **道琼斯工业平均指数**：在纽约证券交易所和纳斯达克（仅次于纽交所的美国第二大证券交易所）交易的 30 只股票的价格加权平均值，用于衡量美国经济中工业部门的业绩。

8. **经济学**：描述在需求无限的世界里有限资源的生产、分配和消费的社会科学。

9. **效率**：在经济学中，效率是指所有的资源达到最优化配置的状态。在证券交易所中，效率意指股票价格最接近其代表的公司的真正价值。

10. **有效市场假说（EMH）**：这一观点认为资产价格，包括股票价格，反映了有关该资产或所属公司所有可知信息。

11. **实证**：可通过观察验证的信息，以及基于此类信息而非理论得出的结论。

12. （美国）联邦储备系统（美联储）：美国中央银行，掌管着美国的货币和金融体系。

13. 2007—2008 年金融崩溃：该事件引发了自 20 世纪 30 年代大萧条以来世界范围内最严重的衰退。事件的起因是与高风险房地产市场（特别是美国地产市场）挂钩的高价证券的快速扩张。全球股市在这次事件中蒸发了数十亿美元。

14. 金融服务业：一个国家的银行、保险公司、信用合作社、房地产公司等企业提供的经济服务。

15. 基本面分析：通过衡量"内在价值"对证券（如债券或股票）进行估值的一种方法。"内在价值"指证券在市场上的真正价值，而非当前的定价。

16. 2007—2009 年的全球经济衰退：自 20 世纪 30 年代大萧条以来世界范围内最严重的衰退。起因是与次级（高风险）房地产市场（尤其是美国地产市场）挂钩的证券快速扩张。该类证券市场的崩溃导致全球主要金融机构破产，各国政府纷纷救市纾困，避免更大的破坏。

17. 大萧条：20 世纪 20 年代的一场灾难性经济衰退，始于美国，迅速蔓延至欧洲，尤其是英国，并持续到 20 世纪 30 年代。

18. 对冲基金：一群投资者共同募集的，然后交由共同合伙人管理的资金。其目的是无论市场上涨或下跌，都使投资者回报最大化。对冲基金通常采用高风险的方法，比如用借来的钱投资。

19. 指数基金 / 指数共同基金：刻意挑选的多样化股票的组合，旨在广泛分散市场风险，力求投资组合的表现拟合股票市场的整体水平。

20. 内幕信息：关于上市公司状况的非公开信息。此类信息通常给公司股票的交易者带来优势。使用内幕信息进行股票交易是非法的。

21. 首次公开募股（IPO）：私营公司第一次发行并对公众出售股票的行为，也称公司"上市"。

22. 现代投资组合理论：旨在使股票、债券或其他资产组合的回报（收益）最大化的一种尝试，通过选择风险相互抵消的各种资产使风险最小化。

23. **共同基金**：一群投资者共同募集的，用于购买股票和债券等各种证券的资金。投资者按照出资比例分享投资所得的利润。

24. **纽约证券交易所**：为了方便投资者交易而设立的一个上市公司市场。该交易所位于纽约，是世界上最大的证券交易所。

25. **庞氏骗局**：对投资者承诺高回报、低风险的欺诈行为。用新投资者注入的资金支付先期投资者的收益。只要有新的投资者加入，早期的投资者就会得到所承诺的回报。除了早期投资者外，所有人都会亏钱。

26. **心理学**：研究人类心理和行为的科学。

27. **定量分析**：通过复杂的数学和统计建模对金融市场进行评估。该方法试图从海量的市场信息中分析出市场的未来表现。

28. **量化宽松**：印制大量钞票，向经济注资，抬高大多数资产的价格，尤其是股票价格的政策。

29. **随机漫步理论**：认为价格不可预测，未来的价格走势与过去的价格波动毫无联系的金融理论。该观点与有效市场假说密切相关。

30. **随机性**：事件或顺序的完全不可预测性。

31. **证券**：一种证明对上市公司具有部分所有权的凭证（股票），或承诺偿付政府机构或公司贷款的金融协议（债券）。

32. **"智能贝塔"策略**：创建已购股票的指数，试图利用市场上的系统性偏见或低效现象的投资方案。

33. **投机者**：马尔基尔认为，投机者是购买股票，希望获得短期收益的人。

34. **股票**：证明投资人对公司具有部分所有权的证券。投资人凭此享有公司未来相应的资产和收益。

35. **次级房地产市场**：房地产市场的低端，涉及那些最无力支付抵押贷款的人。因此，投资次级房地产市场的风险特别高。

36. **系统性风险**：指整个金融市场或整个金融体系崩溃的风险，而非投资于整个金融体系的某一方面（例如某家公司）所涉及的风险。对公司的投资面临的风险通常两者兼有。

37. **技术分析**：通过评估历史价格和交易量，以及其他统计数据来预测证券未来价格的策略。

38. **郁金香球茎热**：17世纪在荷兰新上市（但仍相对稀有）的郁金香球茎的合同价格达到了天文数字，之后崩溃。

39. **先锋集团**：一家美国投资管理公司，是截至2015年3月全球最大的共同基金（主要为指数共同基金）供应方，也是全球第二大交易所交易基金供应方，管理资产逾3万亿美元。

40. **美国次贷危机**：2007—2008年从美国蔓延至全球的金融危机。首先房地产价格大幅下挫，导致众多丧失抵押品赎回权、抵押贷款拖欠现象（尤其是在更贫困的"次贷"市场），最终导致大型银行和金融公司突然破产。随着全球进入经济衰退期，家庭支出也急剧下降。

41. **第二次世界大战**（1939—1945）：轴心国（德国、意大利和日本）与战胜的同盟国（英国及其殖民地、前苏联、美国及其他国家）之间的全球冲突。

人名表

1. 路易·巴舍利耶（1870—1946），法国数学家，常被誉为撰文将高等数学应用到金融研究的第一人。

2. 约翰·C. 博格尔（1929—2019），美国经济学家和投资人，先锋集团的创始人和已退休首席执行官，第一只指数共同基金的创立者。他的畅销书《共同基金常识》（1999）被认为是投资界的经典之作。

3. 沃伦·巴菲特（1930 年生），著名投资人，伯克希尔·哈撒韦投资基金的董事长兼首席执行官，也是世界上最富有的人之一。他将其成功的投资归功于基本面分析，并公开质疑了有效市场假说。

4. 安德莉亚·库姆斯（1965 年生），屡获殊荣的美国记者，个人理财专栏作家和编辑。她认为《漫步华尔街》是对新手投资者而言最重要的一本书。

5. 查尔斯·D. 埃利斯（1937 年生），美国投资顾问，信奉指数共同基金。1975 年他写下"输家的游戏"一文，公开质疑了几乎每一位基金经理的业绩。

6. 尤金·F. 法玛（1939 年生），美国诺贝尔经济学奖得主，关注股市行为分析，以实证证据支持有效市场假说著称。

7. 米尔顿·弗里德曼（1912—2006），美国诺贝尔经济学奖得主，专门从事货币政策研究。他的理论在 20 世纪 80 年代特别有影响力，如今继续影响保守经济政策。

8. 艾伦·格林斯潘（1926 年生），美国央行美联储主席。任职时间为 1987 年到 2006 年。

9. 迈克尔·詹森（1939 年生），美国经济学家，哈佛大学名誉教授，专攻金融领域。

10. 约翰·梅纳德·凯恩斯（1883—1946），英国经济学家。他的宏观经济理论颠覆了经济学领域，为今天的"凯恩斯主义"经济学学派奠定了基础。他信奉技术分析——认为股票价格过去的趋势有助于预测未来走势。

11. **彼得·林奇**（1944年生），投资人。他管理的麦哲伦基金在1977—1990年间取得了29.2％的年均回报率。他持续"战胜了市场"。

12. **保罗·A.萨缪尔森**（1915—2009），第一位获得诺贝尔经济学奖的美国人，被誉为"现代经济学之父"。他在20世纪70年代公开质疑共同基金经理的业绩。

13. **小弗雷德·施韦德**，美国股票经纪人，著有《客户的游艇在哪里？》（1940）一书，公开嘲讽华尔街专业人士的价值。

14. **罗伯特·J.希勒**（1946年生），诺贝尔经济学奖得主，著有《非理性繁荣》（2000）。他通过金融经济学和行为金融学方面的研究对有效市场假说提出质疑。

15. **乔治·索罗斯**（1930年生），世界上最富有、最著名的投资人之一。他是索罗斯基金管理公司的董事长，公开质疑有效市场假说。

16. **纳西姆·尼古拉斯·塔勒布**（1960年生），黎巴嫩裔美国作家和投资人。他对随机性和不确定性的研究对金融和哲学等学科产生了影响。

WAYS IN TO THE TEXT

- Burton G. Malkiel is an American academic and investor who started as an analyst on Wall Street before moving to a very successful academic career.

- *A Random Walk Down Wall Street* argues that movements in stock* market prices are completely unpredictable, or "random."*

- The book is an argument for the efficient market hypothesis* (EMH), according to which no investor can consistently "beat the market," since in today's world, all legally obtained information that can affect stock prices is almost instantly available to all investors.

Who Is Burton G. Malkiel?

Burton G. Malkiel, the author of *A Random Walk Down Wall Street: The Time-Tested Strategy for Successful Investing* (1973) was born in Boston in 1932 and is a well-known American economist, investor, businessman, and writer. He started out as an analyst on Wall Street before quickly moving into academia, earning a PhD in economics* at Princeton University before taking a post in the institution's economics department. Following a distinguished academic career at Princeton, he now holds the title of Chemical Bank Chairman's Professor of Economics Emeritus ("emeritus" means retired).

During his academic career, Malkiel was also active in the business world; he served as director for over a dozen private companies, in the US government as a member of the Council of Economic Advisers (a body that advises the US president), and as president of the American Finance Association.*

But despite all these professional achievements in the worlds of academia and business, Malkiel remains best known for his book *A Random Walk Down Wall Street*. It was first published in 1973 and became a bestseller. It has now run to 11 editions.

The publication of *A Random Walk* thrust Malkiel into the forefront of a debate over whether investment professionals can predict movements in the stock market. He has remained at the center of this debate ever since, publishing many other books and articles in the field of investment theory and practice. He has also created or supported real-life investment products (funds in which investors can put their money, and so on) in line with the conclusions of *A Random Walk*.

What Does *A Random Walk Down Wall Street* Say?

A Random Walk is a book about the stock market—principally the US stock market—which argues that stock prices move in completely random ways. This claim sets its author in instant opposition to the conventional wisdom of Wall Street and its many "experts" (a term that, in the context of financial services—banks, insurance companies, investment funds, and so on—Malkiel can only mock). These experts claim that they can predict the future performance—that is to say, price changes—of stock markets. *A Random Walk* argues directly, and forcefully, against this idea: "Short-run changes in stock prices are unpredictable. Investment advisory services, earnings forecasts, and complicated chart patterns are useless."[1]

In a way, this vision of market "randomness" is a compliment to Wall Street's efficiency.* There is such intense competition among those playing the stock market, Malkiel argues, that there is no real advantage to be gained. So many people are collecting and spreading information that could affect stock prices that there are no (legal) secrets left with which to exploit a "sure thing." Any secret is already out to everyone else, too—except in cases of insider trading* (buying or selling stocks based on confidential information, such as company plans to expand or, on the other hand, plans to announce poor earnings), which is illegal.

As a result, Malkiel claims that every current stock price captures all current available information about the value of the firm in question. This idea, the efficient market hypothesis* (EMH), is more popularly known as the random walk theory.*

The EMH assumes that whenever new information appears that would enable someone to gain a genuine "edge" (the ability to predict before other investors whether an individual stock will go up or down), it spreads to everyone quickly. No single party is able to benefit from it alone. An investor might (legally) receive a piece of news a split second before everyone else, and so make a brilliant investment as a result, but in the long term this is hardly a strategy that will keep working; this is because the stock market "is so good at adjusting to new information that no one can predict its future course in a superior manner. Because of the actions of the pros, the prices of individual stock quickly reflect all the news that is available."[2]

So how does someone invest his or her money, if each

individual stock listed on the stock market is really a crapshoot (just a question of luck)?

One thing that seems certain is the total value of the stock market itself: over decades this has increased significantly, despite peaks and troughs (ups and downs) along the way. Malkiel recommends a "buy-and-hold" strategy of selecting a portfolio* (that is, basket) of stocks so varied that the performance of the whole portfolio of different stocks mirrors that of the stock market average. Over the long term, such an investment seems sure to make significant returns. If you cannot beat the market, it's best to bet on it. In its way, this is a very radical statement—and the last thing Wall Street professionals want the "average investor" to do.

Why Does *A Random Walk Down Wall Street* Matter?

Malkiel's argument has shown remarkable staying power since it first appeared in 1973. For the public, *A Random Walk* provided an intellectual challenge to the value of professional money managers. Not only is it impossible for these managers to consistently beat the market, they also charge customers high fees and high transaction costs each time they buy or sell shares. As a result, even after 11 editions of the book, many professionals in the financial services industry still want to debunk its conclusions. Yet everyone with any interest in the stock market must confront its conclusions. Despite the hostility it has aroused, it has remained popular among investment professionals, financial theorists, and "average investors". Winning a following among this last group is quite an achievement, since "average investors" are so frequently in the grip of investment gurus promising to help them "beat the market."

Through all 11 editions, Malkiel has maintained that *no one* can beat the market reliably over time. Data on the general performance of money managers versus the performance of the stock market itself supports his claim. So his argument is still as relevant as ever. More than four decades after it was first published, *A Random Walk* is still regularly cited, talked about in the financial press and among investment theory academics, and attacked by Wall Street professionals.

Students reading this text will engage with basic questions in the world of investment theory and practice: How and why do stock prices change? Can anyone really "beat the market"? If they cannot, what does this mean for the average investor? According to Malkiel, "There have been so many bewildering claims about the stock market that it's important to have a book that sets the record straight."[3]

It also provides financial know-how, even (or particularly) to the nonspecialist. Malkiel aims to provide "fundamentally a readable investment guide for individual investors."[4] The financial world has become much more sophisticated over the past 40 years. Investment funds now use a dizzying variety of financial instruments, which, technically speaking, can be any kind of tradable asset (including cash), but can even be things such as the debt held by companies or individuals. Malkiel's book is a clear, to-the-point guide through this often confusing world.

This book has remained popular—and hotly disputed—for

over 40 years. Whether or not he is right, it is fair to say Malkiel has succeeded in his goals for *A Random Walk Down Wall Street*— he has made professionals and average investors alike take seriously the idea that you cannot beat the market.

1. Burton G. Malkiel, *A Random Walk Down Wall Street: The Time-Tested Strategy for Successful Investing* (New York: W. W. Norton & Company, 2015), 26.
2. Malkiel, *Random Walk*, 190.
3. Malkiel, *Random Walk*, 18.
4. Malkiel, *Random Walk*, 19.

SECTION 1
INFLUENCES

THE AUTHOR AND THE HISTORICAL CONTEXT

KEY POINTS

* *A Random Walk* bases its analysis on the efficient market hypothesis* (EMH), commonly known as the random walk theory,* according to which the movements of stock* prices are unpredictable.

* The book combines Malkiel's academic understanding of investment theory with his professional financial expertise.

* Challenging fashionable and often very expensive investment strategies, the EMH has provoked spirited debate—especially with investment professionals who make money by claiming they know how to beat the market.

Why Read This Text?

First published in 1973, Burton G. Malkiel's *A Random Walk Down Wall Street: The Time-Tested Strategy for Successful Investing* is now in its 11th edition, and 1.5 million copies have been sold. Promoting the efficient market hypothesis* (EMH)—the principle that the stock market is so efficient* (everything knowable about a company is reflected in its stock price) that future (unknowable) price movements cannot be predicted—it has become a classic in literature related to investment. Malkiel remains a leading figure in academic and financial communities. He still famously believes that "the market prices stocks so efficiently that a blindfolded monkey throwing darts at the stock listings can select a portfolio that performs as well as those managed by the experts."[1]

("Portfolio" here refers to a basket of shares selected to bring a return to an investor.)

The EMH promoted in the book states that security* prices capture all available news and information about their individual companies. "Securities" are commonly things such as stocks or bonds: financial contracts declaring some ownership of a publically traded corporation (stocks), or a promise of repayment for a loan from a corporation or a governmental body (bonds). If a share price does not reflect all available information, then these shares have been priced incorrectly (that is to say, inefficiently). According to the EMH, people will flock to exploit this imbalance (by either buying or selling the incorrectly priced stock) until this inefficiency disappears, and that process tends to happen almost instantly—so quickly that making money from exploiting such inefficiencies over the long term is more or less impossible.

In light of this theory, Malkiel proposes betting on the market itself: by diversifying an investment portfolio (the stocks held) among shares in a great number of companies, the value of the portfolio will match that of the whole stock market. This is called an "index fund,"* which has low operating expenses and low portfolio turnover—few fees paid to professionals and little buying and selling.[2] This incredibly simple strategy almost always outperforms the sophisticated mutual fund managers of Wall Street (the financial district of New York City, and the US money market more generally) over time.

When investors come together to own a diverse portfolio of stocks jointly, which is managed by investment professionals, they invest in "mutual funds."* Always seeking to maximize returns for themselves, mutual fund managers constantly buy and sell stocks for the portfolio—charging high fees and generating capital gains tax* (tax on the increase in the value of the shares) that is payable by their clients along the way.

> "I have been a lifelong investor and successful participant in the market. How successful I will not say, for it is a peculiarity of the academic world that a professor is not supposed to make money."
>
> —— Burton G. Malkiel, *A Random Walk Down Wall Street*

Author's Life

Malkiel was born in Boston in 1932. He graduated from the prestigious Boston Latin School before attending Harvard University, gaining a BA in 1953 and an MBA in 1955. After serving in the Finance Corps of the US Army, Malkiel spent two years as an associate at the former Wall Street investment firm Smith Barney & Company (now part of Morgan Stanley Wealth Management).

In 1960, Malkiel moved from Wall Street to academia, earning a PhD in economics from Princeton University, one of the leading institutions in the United States. He became an assistant professor there, and quickly rose to a chaired professorship (the highest academic post) and head of the economics department. For Malkiel, this move into academia was key to unlocking better investment strategies.

The move cut him off from his former colleagues on Wall

Street, who believe that "academics are so immersed in equations and Greek symbols (to say nothing of stuffy prose) that they couldn't tell a bull from a bear, even in a china shop"[3] (in the language of the stock market, "bulls" are optimistic that prices will rise; "bears" are pessimistic and expect prices to fall). Nonetheless Malkiel also served on the board of directors for a number of companies during this period.

This dual career in business and academia makes Malkiel quite an unusual (and unusually successful) figure. After becoming dean of Yale University's School of Organization and Management in 1981, he eventually returned to Princeton as the Chemical Bank Chairman's Professor of Economics, a post he now holds *in emeritus* (in retirement).

Author's Background

In *A Random Walk*, Malkiel asks a clearly focused question: Is the movement of any company's shares predictable, or are such movements completely random?

If security prices do indeed capture all available news and information about their individual companies, then the future paths of prices can only be random, since they depend entirely on future news: "If an item of news were not random, that is, if it were dependent on an earlier item of news, then it wouldn't be news at all."[4]

By straddling the world of business and academia, Malkiel has a privileged view of how each of these worlds works. Throughout *A Random Walk* he attacks both for obscuring (in his eyes) the simple truth about markets: that they obey the EMH, and that investing in the stock market is therefore a "random walk." In this sense, Malkiel's voice is unique in both the investment world and that of the academic community of investment theory and research.

Malkiel has certainly reached a huge audience in both worlds. The Vanguard Group,* a low-cost index fund investment group where Malkiel served as a director for almost 30 years, now manages over $3 trillion worth of assets. As Malkiel himself notes in *A Random Walk*, since the financial crash of 2007–2008* (an event triggered by the collapse of the highly risky US housing market and the losses incurred by financial institutions that had invested in it), investors endorse his simple strategy more and more: "During 2014, about one-third of the money invested by individuals and institutions was invested in index funds. And that percentage continues to grow."[5]

Although retired, Malkiel remains a productive academic.

---

1. Burton G. Malkiel, *A Random Walk Down Wall Street: The Time-Tested Strategy for Successful Investing* (New York: W. W. Norton & Company, 2015), 19.
2. Malkiel, *Random Walk*, 383.
3. Malkiel, *Random Walk*, 26.
4. Malkiel, *Random Walk*, 155.
5. Malkiel, *Random Walk*, 181.

MODULE 2
ACADEMIC CONTEXT

KEY POINTS

* An academic examination of the stock market, *A Random Walk* considers whether or not its performance can be predicted.

* In the book, Malkiel challenged technical analysis* and fundamental analysis,* two leading approaches that claim to predict stock* price movements; he has continued to challenge newer approaches.

* A number of other economists have come to the same conclusions, both before and after Malkiel's book was published.

The Work in Its Context

Burton G. Malkiel's *A Random Walk Down Wall Street: The Time-Tested Strategy for Successful Investing* introduces a new type of investment analysis called the efficient market hypothesis (EMH),* sometimes referred to as the random walk theory.* The text deals with one of the most basic questions in finance—why prices change in security* markets.[1] ("Securities" are things such as stocks and bonds.)* It states that a stock price captures all available information about the value of a firm, and because of this, there is no way to "beat the market" using legally available information.

Many investors try to take advantage of the gap that frequently exists between a stock's price and its actual value. They try to identify stocks that are undervalued, and expected to increase in value—especially those that will increase more than others.[2] This latter difference is key, because someone who picks stocks that perform better than others "beats the market". Investors often use a dizzying number of forecasting techniques to find such superior returns.[3] But the EMH argues that such advantages cannot exist on a regular basis for anyone.

Few theories have created such passionate debate. The noted Harvard economist Michael Jensen* has said, for example, that "there is no other proposition in economics which has more solid empirical* [data-based] evidence supporting it than the efficient market hypothesis," while the famous investor Peter Lynch* has said, "Efficient markets? That's a bunch of junk, crazy stuff."[4]

> "Markets are not always or even usually correct. But NO ONE PERSON OR INSTITUTION CONSISTENTLY KNOWS MORE THAN THE MARKET."
> —— Burton G. Malkiel, A Random Walk Down Wall Street

Overview of the Field

The field's basic question is whether there is any way to predict the movements of stock prices. This naturally invites an enormous number of opinions from both investors and academic investment theorists, with some arguing that stock prices are predictable while others are convinced that they are not.

The leading views on this subject come from two long-standing schools of thought: "technical analysis" and "fundamental analysis". Malkiel challenges them both.

In simple terms, technical analysis studies past stock prices and volumes of trading in order to predict future prices. For followers of this approach, the market is only 10 percent logical and 90 percent psychological;* they "view the investment game as one of anticipating how the other players will behave."[5]

Fundamental analysis, however, tries to do the opposite— it seeks to remain immune to the optimism and pessimism of the masses. This approach analyzes financial statistics, such as company earnings or asset values, to identify "undervalued" stocks.[6]

Since *A Random Walk* was first published, new schools of thought have emerged. Malkiel has kept pace with all these developments and often examines these new theories with serious academic research. He remains skeptical that any such approaches or "wizardry" can truly work and "beat the market."

Academic Influences

When the French mathematician Louis Bachelier* published *Théorie de la spéculation* (1900), he proclaimed that "the mathematical expectation of the speculator is zero." In other words, an investor who speculates or tries to guess which stocks will perform better cannot expect to make any profit, as losses will always equal gains. Far ahead of his time, Bachelier's study was largely ignored for more than five decades.[7] By the time it was rediscovered, theorists such as the British economist John Maynard Keynes* and the US economist Milton Friedman* had been addressing the same question and had come to similar conclusions.

In 1970, Eugene F. Fama,* an economist from the United

States who went on to win a Nobel Prize in Economic Sciences, published a conclusive paper on the subject. In it he stated that "the evidence in support of the efficient market model is extensive, and (somewhat uniquely in economics) contradictory evidence is sparse."[8]

Along with such mathematical analyses, a growing literature of distrust about the competence of Wall Street professionals appeared. The US stockbroker Fred Schwed Jr.'s* book *Where Are the Customers' Yachts?* (1940) was an early classic of this genre: "Pitifully few financial experts have ever known for two years what was going to happen to any class of securities,"* Schwed wrote. "The majority are usually spectacularly wrong in a much shorter time than that."[9]

More recently, the Nobel Prize-winning economist Robert J. Shiller* published *Irrational Exuberance* (2003), criticizing the market's "positive feedback loops" where price rises encourage more people to buy, raising the price further, until a kind of Ponzi* scheme develops based on mass psychology* rather than fraud[10] (in a Ponzi scheme, early investors receive high rates of return, but when no more investors can be found to inject money, the fraudulent scheme collapses and most participants lose their money). The economist Nassim Nicholas Taleb's* *The Black Swan* (2007) casts empirical* and philosophical doubt on the belief that past stock performance can anticipate future performance.[11] (Empirical evidence is evidence that can be verified by observation.)

A Random Walk's conclusions place it in this tradition

of critical financial literature, backed by Malkiel's serious and ongoing academic research.

---

1. Jonathan Clarke, et al., "The Efficient Markets Hypothesis", *Expert Financial Planning: Investment Strategies from Industry Leaders*, ed. Robert C. Arffa (New York: John Wiley & Sons, 2001), 126.

2. Clarke, "The Efficient Markets Hypothesis", 126.

3. Clarke, "The Efficient Markets Hypothesis", 126.

4. Clarke, "The Efficient Markets Hypothesis", 127.

5. Burton G. Malkiel, *A Random Walk Down Wall Street: The Time-Tested Strategy for Successful Investing* (New York: W. W. Norton & Company, 2015), 110.

6. Burton G. Malkiel, "The Efficient Market Hypothesis and Its Critics", *Journal of Economic Perspectives* 17, no. 1 (winter, 2003): 59.

7. Martin Sewell, "History of the Efficient Market Hypothesis", *UCL Research Note* 11, no. 4 (2011): 2.

8. Eugene F. Fama, "Efficient Capital Markets: A Review of Theory and Empirical Work", *The Journal of Finance* 25, no. 2 (May 1970): 383.

9. Fred Schwed Jr., *Where Are the Customers' Yachts?* (Hoboken: John Wiley & Sons, 2006), 14.

10. Robert J. Shiller, *Irrational Exuberance* (Princeton: Princeton University Press, 2000), 64−8.

11. Nassim Nicholas Taleb, *The Black Swan: The Impact of the Highly Improbable* (London: Penguin, 2007).

THE PROBLEM

KEY POINTS

- The modern idea of an "efficient* market" as applied to stock* exchanges first appeared in a 1965 article published by the US economist Eugene F. Fama.* A radical idea at the time, it challenged the whole value of the financial services industry* and inspired Malkiel to write his book.

- The efficient market hypothesis* (EMH) is opposed by various theories that try to find and exploit patterns in stock price changes.

- The financial collapse of 2007–2008* was perhaps the biggest challenge to the EMH, with some claiming it disproves the hypothesis.

Core Question

The central questions Burton G. Malkiel asks in *A Random Walk Down Wall Street: The Time-Tested Strategy for Successful Investing* are, "Why do stock prices change? How do those changes take place? And is it possible to predict them?" Indeed, these questions are some of the most central to the field of finance altogether.

While on the surface these sound like rational and mathematical problems, the role of emotion in stock markets—particularly the extremes of greed and panic—is not to be underestimated. The British economist John Maynard Keynes* famously said the stock market's movements are due to quirky psychological* factors: "A large proportion of our positive activities depend on spontaneous optimism rather than mathematical expectations," he said.[1] They are dependent on what he called "animal spirits—a spontaneous urge to action rather than inaction."[2] Keynes's conclusion was that "there is nothing so disastrous as a rational investment policy in an irrational world."[3]

The question as to how and why stock prices move remains crucial, and it has a huge impact on both the investor and the entire financial services industry. The end of World War II* in 1945 brought a new era of American economic prosperity, as record amounts of money were invested in the stock market. As a result, the financial sector grew rapidly, with financial professionals all promising superior returns (an obvious impossibility, since it impossible for all to be above average). Since then, there have been numerous, well-known strategies that have all promised to anticipate "what will happen next" on the stock market.

The term "efficient market" first appeared in a 1965 article by Eugene F. Fama,* where he proposed that, "In an efficient market at any point in time the actual price of a security will be a good estimate of its intrinsic (real, core) value."[4] Supporters of EMH insist there is absolutely no way for stock price movements to be predicted. Yet this was a radical idea, prompting Malkiel to write his book challenging the financial services industry and its many claims to almost clairvoyant, far-sighted analyses of stock price movements.

> *"A blindfolded monkey throwing darts at the stock listings could select a portfolio that would do just as well as one selected by the experts."*
> —— Burton G. Malkiel, *A Random Walk Down Wall Street*

The Participants

If stock price movements are driven by some mysterious mixture of logic and emotion, it is perhaps not surprising that the two biggest forecasting camps focus on one side or the other, almost exclusively.

Technical analysts* study past price movements to forecast future ones. They look for any patterns in price movements, based on the idea that the emotional or psychological side of investing, rather than the logical side, drives such shifts. It is a game of studying how other investors in the market behave, in order to anticipate what the crowd will probably do in the future.[5] By contrast, fundamental analysts* try to discover what a stock is really worth, its "true value," in order to exploit the gap between any (inefficiently) low price and a stock's higher true value. Together, these two schools make up a large part of the financial services industry.

Over time, more rivals to the EMH have appeared. Perhaps surprisingly, these have come from within the academic community rather than the business world. One rival is modern portfolio theory.* This states that portfolios of relatively risky stocks can be made much less risky if they are diversified (mixed with other stocks) in the correct way. Another rival, behavioral finance,* has become a rapidly evolving field. It holds that investors are far from rational; it studies behavior such as overconfidence, biased judgments, and herd mentality. The idea is that insights into these factors can enable investors to make money from the gaps they create between stock prices and their true value.

Numerous other financial investment strategies continue to spring up, and many gain huge followings.

The Contemporary Debate

The EMH is more than an idea; intellectually speaking, it is a threat to much of the financial services industry. If it is impossible to beat the market, then why even try?—especially given the high management fees, transaction fees for each purchase or sale of stocks, and the relatively high capital gains tax that becomes payable on any stocks sold for a profit.

Fama's highly regarded research paper "Efficient Capital Markets: A Review of Theory and Empirical Work" (1970) backed the EMH with much real-world research. During the following decade, this model continued to hold sway among investors and economists. It dominated both financial and academic circles, which produced a steady stream of published research to support it.[6] But in the 1980s and 1990s, the EMH began to be questioned by both academics and the business world. For example, research showed that investors regularly overreact or underreact to news— meaning they bid too high or too low for stocks. This alone, at least partially, disproves the EMH.[7]

The economic crash of 2007–2008 was perhaps the greatest challenge to the EMH. Many, including the billionaire hedge-fund manager George Soros,* saw the crisis as having discredited the EMH. After all, certain financial products, in particular those tied to the US subprime real estate market* (risky investments in the housing market) were priced way too high, buoyed by investors' continued decisions to buy in search of high profits. In the end, the bubble*—gross overpricing—burst, and most of those investments became all but worthless.

Addressing the 2007–2008 housing crash head-on, Malkiel says the EMH had indeed worked; the markets ended up finding the correct price for these investments. It just took several years to happen. "The clear conclusion," insists Malkiel, "is that, in every case, the market did correct itself. The market eventually corrects any irrationality."[8]

1. John Maynard Keynes, *The General Theory of Employment, Interest and Money* (London: Macmillan, 1936), 161–2.
2. Keynes, *The General Theory*, 161–2.
3. Milton Friedman and Anna Jacobson Schwartz, *A Monetary History of the United States, 1867–1960* (Princeton: Princeton University Press, 1963), 814.
4. Eugene F. Fama, "Efficient Capital Markets: A Review of Theory and Empirical Work", *The Journal of Finance* 25, no. 2 (May 1970): 383.
5. Burton G. Malkiel, *A Random Walk Down Wall Street: The Time-Tested Strategy for Successful Investing* (New York: W. W. Norton & Company, 2015), 110 –1.
6. Ramy Majouji, "The Financial Markets Context", Open University, accessed November 10, 2015, http://www.open.edu/openlearn/money-management/money/accounting-and-finance/the-financial-markets-context/content-section—acknowledgements.
7. Majouji, "The Financial Markets Context".
8. Malkiel, *Random Walk*, 104.

MODULE 4
THE AUTHOR'S CONTRIBUTION

KEY POINTS

* In *A Random Walk*, Malkiel presents much evidence and actual trading data to demolish the various investing theories that claim they can perform better than the stock* market average.

* By translating the theoretical efficient market hypothesis* (EMH) into a real-life investment strategy—by promoting index funds,* which bet on the rise in the value of the market as a whole rather on the value of individual shares—Malkiel influenced the world of investing as few others have.

* Although largely developed by other academics such as the Nobel Prize-winning economist Eugene F. Fama,* Malkiel took the theory further and popularized it.

Author's Aims

Burton G. Malkiel's aims in writing *A Random Walk Down Wall Street: The Time-Tested Strategy for Successful Investing* were admirably simple. First, he wanted to prove the validity of the efficient market hypothesis (EMH), which states that prices of securities* (like stocks and bonds) capture all available news and information about the companies that issue them. He has a wealth of data and evidence, including stock prices over time, that he elegantly presents. Malkiel then aims to disprove the challengers to the EMH, one by one, particularly the long-standing schools of technical analysis* and fundamental analysis.* He also aims to disprove newer, fashionable investment strategies such as modern portfolio theory* (an approach in which investors minimize risks by choosing assets whose risks offset each other) and, despite acknowledging the valuable insights it has produced, is generally critical of the growing academic field of behavioral finance* (which explores the psychological* characteristics of market participants to explain market movements). "Imagine," he says, "a whole new field in which to publish papers, give lectures for hefty fees, and write graduate theses."[1]

Malkiel aims to show that after taking into account the heavy fees, transaction costs, and tax burdens that come with all "actively managed" strategies (strategies based on frequently buying and selling stocks), the average investor is much better off simply betting on the market itself by investing in an index fund made up of a variety of stocks and then waiting. An index fund is a portfolio of diverse stocks, selected to allow its performance to mirror that of the overall stock market.

Finally, Malkiel aims to provide a full financial guide to his reader. *A Random Walk* offers a broad range of financial advice useful to the average investor, ranging from insurance, to paying for a child's education, to (legal) tax avoidance.

> "I am not promising you stock-market miracles. Indeed, a subtitle for this book might well have been 'The Get Rich Slowly but Surely Book'."
> —— Burton G. Malkiel, *A Random Walk Down Wall Street*

Approach

While the economist Eugene F. Fama is often thought of as the father of the EMH, *A Random Walk* presented these academic findings to the nonspecialist reader. When the book was published (1973), a general awareness was growing that most "actively managed" mutual funds* (money pooled by a number of investors and managed by professionals who buy and sell securities on behalf of those investors) were not performing better than the stock market itself. Malkiel cited the theoretical EMH to make an appeal in *A Random Walk*'s first edition: "What we need is a ... minimum management-fee mutual fund [in which the investor is not charged for buying and selling shares] that simply buys the hundreds of stocks making up the broad stock-market averages and does no trading from security to security in an attempt to catch the winners."[2] He called, in other words, for an "index mutual fund": a portfolio of stocks so diverse that it performs similarly to the overall stock market.

Through the EMH, *A Random Walk* calls for a very practical, long-term approach that was already being followed elsewhere. The market theorist John C. Bogle* founded the US investment management company the Vanguard Group* the year after *A Random Walk*'s publication, and in 1976 created the world's first index mutual fund that was available to the regular investor. While Bogle had many inspirations for this revolutionary index fund, and had long been interested in this approach, it was Malkiel and *A Random Walk* that voiced its goals most clearly to the general public. In 1977, Malkiel himself joined the board of directors of the Vanguard Group, where he served for 28 years. This group is now one of the largest mutual fund companies in the world, with over

$3 trillion in total assets under management. While Vanguard's pioneering index fund was widely mocked when it started in 1974 for not even *trying* to beat the market, index mutual funds are now considered to be the industry standard. *A Random Walk* became the popular intellectual justification for the growth of such funds.

Contribution in Context

When Fama published his groundbreaking paper "Efficient Capital Markets: A Review of Theory and Empirical Work" in 1970, his research confirmed what many others had been thinking for some time.[3] At Princeton University, for example, Bogle's thesis title had been "Mutual Funds can make no claims to superiority over the Market Averages" (1951). Other influential studies closely followed the publication of *A Random Walk* in 1973. The influential economist Paul A. Samuelson's[*] 1974 paper "Challenge to Judgment," for example, famously declared that "superior investment performance is unproved."[4] The US investment consultant Charles D. Ellis's[*] 1975 article "The Loser's Game" reached a similar conclusion: "The investment management business (it should be a profession but is not) is built upon a simple and basic belief: Professional money managers can beat the market. This premise appears to be false."[5] Like Malkiel, Ellis recommends an indexed fund and an acceptance by investors that the market average is the best they can hope for in the stock market as "If you can't beat the market, you certainly should consider joining it."[6]

Even if Malkiel's views in *A Random Walk* were not original or unique at the time, his key contribution to the field still cannot be underestimated. Few theorists have made a bigger impact in the world of investment; his book made the ideas so much more popular on a wide scale, changing the investment world and helping to invent a new type of mutual fund. The debate it has inspired about "beating the market" has continued for over 40 years.[7]

1. Burton G. Malkiel, *A Random Walk Down Wall Street: The Time-Tested Strategy for Successful Investing*, (New York: W. W. Norton & Company, 2015), 230.
2. Malkiel, *Random Walk*, 226–7.
3. Eugene F. Fama, "Efficient Capital Markets: A Review of Theory and Empirical Work", *The Journal of Finance* 25, no. 2 (May 1970).
4. Paul A. Samuelson, "Challenge to Judgment", *The Journal of Portfolio Management* 1, no. 1 (1974): 17.
5. Charles D. Ellis, "The Loser's Game", *The Financial Analysts Journal* 31, no. 4 (July/August 1975): 19.
6. Ellis, "The Loser's Game", 26.
7. "Investment Greats: Burton Malkiel", The Motley Fool, accessed November 21, 2015, http://news.fool.co.uk/news/investing/2011/01/04/investment-greats-burton-malkiel.aspx.

SECTION 2
IDEAS

MAIN IDEAS

KEY POINTS

- Malkiel has two key themes in *A Random Walk:* the efficient market hypothesis (EMH),* and the "smart" way to invest by betting on the stock market as a whole rather than on individual stocks.*

- The book uses data to show that a broad-based index fund,* reflecting the value of the stock market as a whole, has historically performed better than any other strategy for stock market investing.

- Malkiel uses straightforward and accessible language to argue forcefully why his investment approach is better than speculating*—roughly, betting—on short-term profits.

Key Themes

There are two main themes that run through Burton G. Malkiel's *A Random Walk Down Wall Street: The Time-Tested Strategy for Successful Investing.* The first is the efficient market hypothesis; the second is the key distinction between "speculation" and "investment."

According to the random walk theory,* stock prices move in completely unpredictable ways. The market rests on the efficient market hypothesis, being "so efficient—prices move so quickly when information arises—that no one can buy or sell fast enough to benefit. And real news develops randomly, that is, unpredictably."[1] The investor's central question then arises: How can you estimate a stock's "true value" to ensure that you do not overpay when buying shares, or how can you buy something undervalued so that you can "beat the market"?[2]

As Malkiel puts it bluntly many times: this is impossible. No investor can beat the market over the long term, as "The odds of selecting superior stocks or anticipating the general direction of the market are even. Your guess is as good as that of the ape, your stockbroker, or even mine."[3]

Once this fact (in Malkiel's eyes, at least) is agreed, the true "investor" can use the EMH to invest his or her money wisely. This is done by simply betting on the market itself through a broad-based index fund (a fund that buys a wide variety of stocks and then keeps them). That way, the returns on an investment mirror those of the stock market as a whole over the long term, which practically guarantees major gains. Only the foolish "speculator" continues to aim for superior returns in the short term. As the market is a "random walk", this is impossible to keep up—something the EMH makes obvious, but which those working in the investment business will always deny (for obviously self-interested reasons: to protect the fees they earn managing people's money, having promised them earnings higher than the average increase in stock value).

> "Anomalies can crop up, markets can get irrationally optimistic, and often they attract unwary investors. But, eventually, true value is recognized by the market, and this is the main lesson investors must heed."
> —— Burton G. Malkiel, *A Random Walk Down Wall Street*

Exploring the Ideas

A Random Walk argues that the EMH holds true in real stock markets, including the New York stock exchange.* If this were not true, it would be much easier to "beat the market," but Malkiel shows convincingly how difficult this would be to achieve: "An investor with $10,000 at the start of 1969 who invested in a Standard & Poor's 500-Stock Index Fund would have had a portfolio worth $736,196 by June 2014, assuming that all dividends were reinvested. A second investor who instead purchased shares in the average actively managed fund would have seen his investment grow to $501,470. The difference is dramatic."[4]

That is to say, the index fund, which invests broadly and in accordance with the EMH (it simply buys shares in a wide variety of companies) does almost 1.5 times as well as the fund managed by "expert" investment managers. This timespan includes many "up" and "down" years for the stock market, but over the long term the index mutual fund still does much better. These figures clearly show that, given enough time, Wall Street is able to deliver on its promises, and point toward a smarter way of investing. So why don't more people simply put their money into a long-term index mutual fund? The answer is that many people are more interested in "speculating" than "investing", a key difference made in *A Random Walk*.

An investor, in Malkiel's eyes, "buys stocks likely to produce a dependable future stream of cash returns and capital gains when measured over years or decades."[5] In contrast, Malkiel has little time for the speculator, who "buys stocks hoping for a short-term gain over the next few days or weeks."[6] Malkiel argues against such speculation, which often buys into the momentum of rising stocks to make a quick profit. He calls this the "Madness of Crowds." Starting with the Tulip Bulb Craze* in seventeenth-century Holland (when competition pushed up the price of tulip bulbs to astronomical levels, a situation that was soon followed by a price collapse), Malkiel summarizes a series of similar "bubbles"* that eventually proved disastrous for investors who bought into them. His point remains clear throughout: "Invariably, the hottest stocks or fund in one period are the worst performers in the next."[7] The very common desire to get rich quick makes such speculators easy prey for Wall Street's promises of "market-beating" strategies. In a way, Malkiel completely agrees with the financial fraudster Charles Ponzi (creator of the Ponzi scheme,* where high rates of return are promised to investors, which are paid out from the money provided by new investors) who once said that "When a man's vision is fixed on one thing, he might as well be blind."[8]

Malkiel then reviews many different forms of these active investment strategies ("active" in that they involve buying and selling stocks much more often than in the passive approach he advocates) that still claim to "beat the market". They include technical analysis* (which examines past price trends to predict future ones) and fundamental analysis* (which seeks to find the "true value" of a stock). He also examines modern portfolio theory,* which tries to balance risky stocks against each other, and the new field of behavioral finance,* which examines the psychological* side to investing (like "herd behavior"—the influence of mass psychology). Malkiel finds some insights in this relatively new field, though he views them as being quite limited.

Malkiel's conclusion is clear and consistent: "The core of every investment portfolio should consist of low-cost, tax-efficient, broad-based index funds," which guarantee market return.[9]

Language and Expression

Malkiel aims to provide the reader with an easily accessible guide to investment and finance, including discussion of academic advances in investment theory and practice.[10] He matches his insights into complex investment models with clear explanations. His style is conversational, informal, friendly, and at times even humorous. For example, at one point he states that, "If your broker calls to say that IPO (initial public offering*) shares will be available to you, you can bet that the new issue is a dog"[11]— that is, not especially valuable. Sometimes, however, he adopts a more professorial tone that some might find off-putting, or even patronizing. "[T]he conscientious reader will now note that in the schematic illustration..." he writes at one point that, for example, before presenting the reader with information.[12]

What often makes Malkiel's ideas so strong is not their originality so much as the way he expresses them. Simple points, like the importance of not panicking and selling shares when their prices fall unexpectedly, have a big impact in Malkiel's hands: "A buy-and-hold investor would have seen one dollar invested in the Dow Jones Industrial Average* [an average of 30 stocks traded on the New York stock exchange*] in 1900 grow to $290 by the start of 2013. Had that investor missed the best five days each year, however, that dollar investment would have been worth less than a penny in 2013."[13]

1. Burton G. Malkiel, *A Random Walk Down Wall Street: The Time-Tested Strategy for Successful Investing* (New York: W. W. Norton & Company, 2015), 184.
2. Malkiel, *Random Walk*, 105.
3. Malkiel, *Random Walk*, 190.
4. Malkiel, *Random Walk*, 17.
5. Malkiel, *Random Walk*, 28.
6. Malkiel, *Random Walk*, 28.
7. Malkiel, *Random Walk*, 254.
8. Douglas H. Dunn, *Ponzi* (New York: McGraw-Hill, 1975), 134.
9. Malkiel, *Random Walk*, 261.
10. Malkiel, *Random Walk*, 18.
11. Malkiel, *Random Walk*, 257.
12. Malkiel, *Random Walk*, 214.
13. Malkiel, *Random Walk*, 157.

SECONDARY IDEAS

KEY POINTS

* Malkiel examines "new investment technology"—theories and strategies of investment—in some detail; but he is not convinced of their usefulness.

* Increased risk cannot be managed by diversification (buying a spread of different stocks* to create a diverse portfolio) given the "systemic risks"* that Malkiel explores.

* Some big questions are left unanswered by Malkiel, such as what would happen if another asset bubble,* such as the one that caused the financial crash of 2007–2008,* should burst: could the stock market itself survive it?

Other Ideas

The 11th edition of Burton G. Malkiel's *A Random Walk Down Wall Street: The Time-Tested Strategy for Successful Investing* gives "technical"* and "fundamental"* analyses short shrift before moving on to newer trends. He gives a thorough examination of what he sarcastically calls "the rarified world of 'new investment technology' created within the towers of the academy" and often followed today in the world of investment.[1]

Among the newer trends, Malkiel first explores modern portfolio theory,* which tries to balance risk in an overall portfolio to produce superior returns. He also examines the "capital-asset pricing model," which basically claims that you *must* increase the total level of risk in a portfolio to earn superior returns. To do this in "the right way" requires following a method mysteriously labeled "beta."[2] The mathematical calculation for "beta" in a stock captures the sensitivity of its price to general market movements.

Malkiel also reviews behavioral finance.* This approach studies irrational market behavior, including biased judgments, herd mentality, overconfidence, and loss aversion (a desire to avoid losses) in order to make money from the gaps these behaviors create between stock prices and their actual value. Despite finding much to fault in this model, Malkiel draws many insights from it that further inform his own "random walk" model.*

Finally, Malkiel provides a "Practical Guide for Random Walkers and Other Investors" that shows how to put his random walk model to work in all aspects of your personal finances.

"In investing, we are often our worst enemy."
—— Burton G. Malkiel, *A Random Walk Down Wall Street*

Exploring the Ideas

Modern portfolio theory attempts to combine various riskier—and potentially higher-earning—stocks in ways that balance these risks against each other. For example, someone interested in an island economy might invest in both a large beach resort and an umbrella manufacturer in order to make money no matter what the island's weather.[3] The problem, according to Malkiel, is that the fortunes of most companies tend to move in the same direction. "When there is a recession and people are unemployed, they may buy neither summer vacations nor umbrellas. Therefore, one shouldn't expect in practice to get the neat kind of risk elimination just shown."[4]

This holds true in events such as the global economic recession of 2007–2009,* when all markets fell at the same time. Those holding the riskiest stocks experienced the worst losses, no matter how they had been combined. This prompted Malkiel to comment, "Small wonder that some investors came to believe that diversification no longer seemed to be effective as a strategy against risk."[5]

Investors have invented a number of "smart beta" strategies* (mathematical formulas that try to capture market inefficiencies), which in general means trying to achieve higher returns with no increased risk.[6] Malkiel doubts the value of any of these strategies, writing, "Despite the mathematical manipulations involved, the basic idea behind the beta measurement is one of putting some precise numbers on the subjective feelings money managers have had for years." In other words, complex math is actually being used to support "hunches" or general opinions gleaned from far less objective sources.[7]

Again, Malkiel finds that this theory falls apart on the rocks of "systemic risk"—the tendency for all stocks to go along with the general market.[8] As in his discussion of modern portfolio theory, he shows that such systemic risk (that is, the risk that the whole market will drop in value) "cannot be eliminated by diversification" (spreading the risk by buying a suite of shares, for example). He also uses this logic to dismiss all models that try to determine the core value of different shares ("capital-asset pricing models"), which may be different from the price at which they are trading. This is because even if such a "pricing inefficiency" is discovered (that is, share prices do not reflect the real value of a company), they are sure to be corrected almost instantly as other investors observe the same thing: "Investors would snap at the chance to have these higher returns, bidding up the prices of stocks" that the models had correctly identified as being underpriced.[9]

Regarding behavioral finance, Malkiel disagrees completely with its belief that irrational behavior can lead to share prices that are too high or too low. "Efficient-market theory believers assert that smart rational traders will correct any mispricings that might arise from the presence of irrational traders."[10] But Malkiel also admits that the insights of behavioral finance can help the average investor "quite a bit".[11] Learning about these disruptive, irrational dynamics is a good thing for any investor (even if the all-knowing market will eventually weed them out).

Overlooked

Much academic literature supports Malkiel's EMH. As Malkiel says repeatedly in *A Random Walk*, asset bubbles (a term describing the increase in price of a stock or other asset beyond its actual value) must eventually be self-correcting. Investors will realize that prices cannot go any higher, and then a massive sell-off will take place. This abrupt sale will then cause the collapse of a company's share price and bring it down closer to its actual value.

But Malkiel never addresses whether the market itself is strong enough to deal with these ever-bigger crashes. When bubbles burst on the scale of the 2007–2008 subprime mortgage crisis* (a financial crisis founded on the trading of risky mortgages in the

United States), government bailouts were required to preserve the very existence of the stock market. It is a clear and present danger that these crashes are getting bigger over time, rather than being isolated catastrophes. For example, the global financial meltdown of 2007–2008 can be seen as "just the most recent installment in a recurrent pattern of financial overreach, taxpayer bailout, and subsequent Wall Street ingratitude. And all indications are that the pattern is set to continue."[12]

It is not absurd to suggest that a crash will occur of such size that the government will not be able to bail out the stock market, and investors will lose everything—even those "wise" investors who put their money in broad-based index funds, but Malkiel never addresses this possibility.

1. Burton G. Malkiel, *A Random Walk Down Wall Street: The Time-Tested Strategy for Successful Investing* (New York: W. W. Norton & Company, 2015), 189.
2. Malkiel, *Random Walk*, 210.
3. Malkiel, *Random Walk*, 197–9.
4. Malkiel, *Random Walk*, 199.
5. Malkiel, *Random Walk*, 204.
6. Malkiel, *Random Walk*, 260–1.
7. Malkiel, *Random Walk*, 210.
8. Malkiel, *Random Walk*, 210.
9. Malkiel, *Random Walk*, 215.
10. Malkiel, *Random Walk*, 230.
11. Malkiel, *Random Walk*, 230.
12. Paul Krugman and Robin Wells, "The Busts Keep Getting Bigger: Why?", *The New York Review of Books*, July 14, 2011, accessed February 16, 2016, http://www.nybooks.com/articles/2011/07/14/busts-keep-getting-bigger-why/.

MODULE 7
ACHIEVEMENT

KEY POINTS

* In promoting the efficient market hypothesis* (EMH), Malkiel argued that almost every aspect of the conventional wisdom of the world of investment is nonsense. Readers and investors have responded positively to his message for over 40 years.

* *A Random Walk* put together and further developed a number of trends in investment theory from the early 1970s, mainly those based around the EMH.

* The 2007–8 financial crash* challenged Malkiel's approach; while critics say the price bubble* linked to the housing market shows the market had not found the right price for those assets, Malkiel says the model worked—it just took a few years for the bubble to burst before prices returned to the right level.

Assessing the Argument

When writing *A Random Walk Down Wall Street: The Time-Tested Strategy for Successful Investing*, Burton G. Malkiel's intention was clear: "There have been so many bewildering claims about the stock market that it's important to have a book that sets the record straight."[1] In this context, "setting the record straight" means accepting the idea that stock market prices reflect all currently available information about the stocks. The patterns of a stock's* past price movements will tell you nothing about its future movements, and the "true value" of a stock at any given time is always an estimate and never precise. Only the market (over time) reveals which stocks have a growing core value (as reflected by a rising price), and which do not.

These ideas were born both from trends in investment theory in the late 1960s to early 1970s and the efficient market hypothesis (EMH). They have proved remarkably durable since then, as has the popularity of *A Random Walk*. The preface to the 11th edition of 2015 reflects just how solidly Malkiel's analysis has stood up to a rapidly changing world; the long list of things that did not exist when the first edition was published in 1973 includes everyday features of the financial landscape such as automatic teller machines, a number of modern trading techniques, mutual funds,* and tax-exempt funds—"to mention just a few of the changes that have occurred in the financial environment."[2]

Nonetheless, in this new world of complicated investment strategies, Malkiel remains certain about the EMH: "Now, over forty years later, I believe even more strongly in that original thesis."[3]

This statement is both popular and credible—and taken as gospel by investors with trillions of dollars invested in broad-based index mutual funds.* It is a reflection of Malkiel's extraordinary achievement.

> *"Talk to 10 money experts and you're likely to hear 10 recommendations for Burton Malkiel's classic investing book."*
> ——Andrea Coombes*, *The Wall Street Journal*

Achievement in Context

A Random Walk was first published in 1973 and addressed an entirely different era on Wall Street: one in which the EMH had recently been proved true by empirical* (data-based) evidence (as expressed in Eugene F. Fama's* landmark 1970 article "Efficient Capital Markets: A Review of Theory and Empirical Work").[4] The EMH was becoming generally accepted among investment theorists. Likewise, in the real-life investment community the EMH and its implications were gaining ground: John Bogle* founded the Vanguard Group in 1974 and offered the first index mutual fund soon after. Malkiel's book was a central part of this movement, and made these ideas accessible to the nonspecialist, "average" investor.

Over the past 42 years Malkiel has regularly updated *A Random Walk*, with the new editions addressing new investment theories and practices. Meanwhile, an increasing number of academics and investors have challenged Malkiel's conclusions, creating a lively dialogue between those who still believe they can "actively" manage money to "beat the market," and voices like Malkiel who believe in the "passive" strategy of long-term investment in an index mutual fund.[5] However, the financial crash of 2007–2008 in which the housing and stock markets collapsed— the worst crisis since the Great Depression* of the 1920s and 1930s— has perhaps produced new evidence that discredits the EMH on theoretical and practical grounds. This remains an ongoing debate.

Limitations

A Random Walk remains famous in the world of investment theory and practice and, as academics have increasingly questioned the random walk model,* Malkiel has remained its most vocal defender. In 2003, he wrote that "By the start of the twenty-first century, the intellectual dominance of the efficient market hypothesis had become far less universal. Many financial economists and statisticians began to believe that stock prices are at least partially predictable."[6]

Malkiel accepts that because of irrational or mistaken judgment by investors, "pricing irregularities and even predictable patterns in stock returns can appear over time and even persist for short periods." Yet he does not think such inefficiencies can last for any length of time—certainly not long enough to provide investors with a strategy for obtaining superior returns.[7]

The crash of 2007–2008 provides a tough test for the EMH. For several years leading up to the crash, banks and other financial companies had been creating and selling various securities* based on housing mortgages. The prices of these investment instruments continued to rise until the crash, when many lost most or all of their value. Yet, in an "efficient" market, how could these assets have been so dramatically overpriced? Many felt the crash made the EMH obsolete because "the markets didn't work."[8] For Malkiel, this skepticism simply showed a misunderstanding of the EMH: "What the efficient market hypothesis does not mean is that markets are always correct," he said in a 2012 television interview, with reference to the crash.[9] "Markets are always wrong. The point is nobody knows at any one time—the price is wrong, but nobody knows whether it's too high or too low and the market is unbeatable, but that doesn't mean it's right."[10]

For Malkiel, the market only "gets it right" over the long term: once the bubble burst in 2007–2008, assets and share prices went back down to a closer approximation of their real value. Once again, the fact that bubbles *do* burst is strong evidence, in Malkiel's eyes, that the EMH holds true.

Ultimately, *A Random Walk* depends on empirical data (records of actual trading prices, rather than theories) from stock markets. If the data cease to back up the EMH, then the text will find itself disproven. So far the EMH has held true over the long term. But it is much more limited in the short or medium term—or when violent fluctuations occur, like the 2007–2008 crash, which can threaten the entire financial system.

1. Burton G. Malkiel, *A Random Walk Down Wall Street: The Time-Tested Strategy for Successful Investing* (New York: W. W. Norton & Company, 2015), 18.
2. Malkiel, *Random Walk*, 18.
3. Malkiel, *Random Walk*, 17.
4. Ramy Majouji, "The Financial Markets Context", Open University, accessed February 16, 2016, http://www.open.edu/openlearn/money-management/money/accounting-and-finance/the-financial-markets-context/content-section—acknowledgements.
5. Malkiel, *Random Walk*, 254.
6. Burton G. Malkiel, "The Efficient Market Hypothesis and its Critics", *Journal of Economic Perspectives* 17, no. 1 (2003): 60.
7. Malkiel, "The Efficient Market Hypothesis and its Critics", 80.
8. Sam Ro, "Finance Wizard Burton Malkiel Defends the Efficient Market Hypothesis", accessed November 25, 2015, http://www.businessinsider.com/burton-malkiel-efficient-market-hypothesis-2012-4?IR=T.
9. Ro, "Finance Wizard Burton Malkiel".
10. Ro, "Finance Wizard Burton Malkiel".

PLACE IN THE AUTHOR'S WORK

KEY POINTS

- Malkiel's primary focus throughout his life's work has been the efficient market hypothesis* (EMH), or random walk theory,* and how to apply it to real-life stock* markets.
- For Malkiel, the "closed-end fund,"* which raises its capital only once by issuing a fixed number of shares, is the only type of actively traded fund that might reward investment.
- Although Malkiel has written many other books on different aspects of investment theory and practice, *A Random Walk* remains by far the best known and most studied.

Positioning

By the time *A Random Walk Down Wall Street: The Time-Tested Strategy for Successful Investing* was published in 1973, Burton G. Malkiel was already a leading American academic, with a professorship in economics at Princeton University. He had published books on international monetary policy, interest rate structures, and securities* options as well as a great number of influential articles. Nonetheless, *A Random Walk* became the high point of his career, and was soon a national best seller. It remains one of the most talked-about and debated texts in both academia and the professional financial services community.

A Random Walk is also an ongoing achievement: Malkiel has published 11 editions of the book, each largely different from those that came before. Every new edition has addressed the latest theories challenging the EMH, as well as new, more practical challenges from the day's business landscape. Accordingly, the heart of each edition has remained essentially the same, both in its theoretical conclusion—that the EMH holds—and its investment advice—guiding the reader towards broad-based index mutual funds.* While the 2007–2008 crash* and the global economic recession* have damaged the reputation of many investment strategies, Malkiel's approach in *A Random Walk* has been strengthened: investors can only be protected from such shocks by focusing on the long term.

> *"One of the most rewarding features for me in writing eleven editions of this book has been the many letters I have received from grateful investors. They tell me how much they have benefited from following the simple advice that has remained the same for forty years. Those timeless lessons involve broad diversification, annual rebalancing, using index funds, and staying the course."*
> —— Burton G. Malkiel, *A Random Walk Down Wall Street*

Integration

Malkiel has had a remarkably varied career as both an academic and professional investment advisor. Since 1973 he has not only published 10 further editions of *A Random Walk*, but also a great number of other books and articles on different aspects of investing: how endowed institutions should manage risk (these are colleges or other nonprofit bodies in possession of a sum of donated money, known as an endowment. Generally only the interest earned from the endowment may be spent); beating inflation as an investor; and the structure of share prices, to name just a few.

Malkiel's main message in *A Random Walk* is that the best investment strategy is generally to place money in an index mutual fund*—a fund that pools the money of numerous investors and then buys stocks from a wide range of companies and holds on to them for a long time, so achieving the same long-term growth in value as the stock market as a whole. This buy-and-hold—or "passive"—investing approach also involves lower management fees than a mutual fund, which uses an "active" approach of frequent buying and selling in search of short-term profits.

While Malkiel generally disapproves of active investing, he makes an exception for one type: the "closed-end fund".[1] This preference emerged in his influential 1977 article "The Valuation of Closed-End Investment Company Shares", where he explores the opportunities presented by these unique funds.

Closed-end funds are actively managed, like mutual funds, but are structured entirely differently, and in a way that appeals to Malkiel despite being a departure from his usual exhortations for the passive-fund strategy. While most mutual funds can take on an increasing number of investors, a closed-end fund issues a fixed number of shares at the beginning to raise its capital in one go. This is what a company does in an initial public offering (IPO),* when it makes its shares available to the public for the first time; but in this case, the shares do not represent ownership in a company but participation in a "closed-end fund". Crucially, the price of these closed-end shares is not only a reflection of the assets the fund possesses and manages, but also a reflection of how many investors want to buy shares in it at the time.[2]

Sometimes the demand for shares in a closed-end fund is lower than that demanded by the market value of the fund's assets. In such cases, the price for the shares may be lower than it should be. This lower price represents an effective discount for those who do buy in at that price. If you buy shares in such a fund at such a discount and its assets match the overall performance of the market, you will in effect be gaining superior returns, since you bought in low.[3] That Malkiel still agrees with this analysis in the 2015 edition of *Random Walk* speaks to the solid ground of its conclusions.

It could be argued that all Malkiel's published works, even the influential "Valuation of Closed-End Investment Company Shares", are overshadowed by the huge achievement that is *A Random Walk*. As many of his other works provide additional commentary on and analysis of his random walk theory, his body of work can be considered highly coherent and unified.

Significance

While Malkiel was already a highly influential academic and successful investor, it is fair to say that *A Random Walk* is his best and most important work. Although the EMH was defined and demonstrated with empirical* data by the Nobel Prize-winning economist Eugene F. Fama,* Malkiel's books became the popular intellectual justification for long-term investment in broad-based index mutual funds, now a trillion-dollar business. The book's influence in investment theory and practice cannot be overestimated. He has been both praised and denounced by leading academic minds and famous billionaire investors such as the Americans George Soros* and Warren Buffett.*4 The book has been cited thousands of times.

A Random Walk still defines Malkiel's reputation, despite his other published work. Some of the other subjects he has written about have a big presence in his theoretical and investing outlook, such as his focus on closed-end fund discounts, but in the public mind this is a small footnote to his random walk model. This theory asks the biggest of all questions when it comes to stocks: Can you predict what the market will do and so steadily earn superior returns on your investment? The entire financial industry has always said, and must always say, that you absolutely can if you're smart enough. Malkiel reached a popular audience with the message that beating the market is impossible. Because he has a huge body of sophisticated evidence to support this position, and was able to communicate it in accessible terms, Malkiel is the natural target for those experts and rival academics who want to attack the random walk theory and prove that stock prices *are* predictable.

Of particular significance was the makeup of the audience Malkiel reached with the text: the kind of "average investors" who are, he claims, constantly fleeced by Wall Street professionals claiming to possess insight that, in reality, cannot exist.

1. Burton G. Malkiel, *A Random Walk Down Wall Street: The Time-Tested Strategy for Successful Investing* (New York: W. W. Norton & Company, 2015), 401.
2. Burton G. Malkiel, "The Valuation of Closed-End Investment Company Shares", *Journal of Finance* 32, no. 3 (June 1977): 847.
3. Malkiel, "The Valuation of Closed-End Investment Company Shares", 858.
4. For examples, see George Soros, "Soros: Financial Markets", *Financial Times*, October 17, 2009, accessed February 19, 2016, http://www.ft.com/intl/cms/s/2/dbc0e0c6-bfe9-11de-aed2-00144feab49a.html#axzz40d8gJIsO; and Warren Buffet, "The Superinvestors of Graham and Doddsville", *Hermes*, Columbia Business School Magazine, May 17, 1984.

SECTION 3
IMPACT

THE FIRST RESPONSES

KEY POINTS

* Although critics have claimed that price inefficiencies do exist in the stock* market and can be exploited for gain (that is, that it is possible to predict and exploit price fluctuations in the market), Malkiel says that in the long run, such inefficiencies disappear, so the efficient market hypothesis* (EMH) approach is still better.

* The world's most prominent investor, Warren Buffett,* maintains that there is much inefficiency in the market to be exploited; his successful investment record is compelling proof.

* Malkiel admits that price bubbles* have existed for centuries— but argues that although this is clearly irrational and inefficient market behavior, in the long term, bubbles burst and markets are efficient.

Criticism

The critical response to Burton G. Malkiel's *A Random Walk Down Wall Street: The Time-Tested Strategy for Successful Investing* has been mostly positive, particularly as research continues to show that stock markets are indeed efficient.[1] "Efficient" here means that the markets will find a price for each stock that accurately reflects all known information about the company it represents; if publically available information indicates that a company is doing well—or poorly—investors will bid the price of its stock up, or down. However, since the 1970s, the intellectual authority of the EMH has come under increasing attack as many financial economists and statisticians have come to believe that stock prices are at least partially predictable.[2]

One leading critical study by business researchers from the Massachusetts Institute of Technology (MIT) and the University of Pennsylvania was published with the (slightly mocking) title *A Non-Random Walk Down Wall Street* (1999). It challenged Malkiel's argument by showing mathematically that inefficiencies *do* exist in the stock market and can be exploited by active investors.[3] In the 11th edition of *A Random Walk*, Malkiel is happy to admit this point: "The stock market does not conform perfectly to the mathematician's ideal of the complete independence of present price movements from those of the past."[4] But his response is, so what? "The systematic relationships that exist are often so small that they are not useful to investors," he writes—they will be outweighed by the fees and capital gains tax* that come with frequent transactions.[5] In other words, it may sometimes happen that the stock price of a company that has performed strongly in the past will continue to rise more often than it will fall, simply due to investors' expectations. But such "predictable" movements are likely to be small and if you give your money to investment professionals to try to take advantage of such distortions, the fees they charge will tend to wipe out any gains they can generate for you.

Other critics have argued that investors go through waves of excess optimism and pessimism, causing stock prices to deviate (go further up or down) in noticeable ways.[6] Other critics have detected "seasonal or day of the week" patterns; trading in January, for example, seems to take on certain regular features.[7] Indeed, Eugene F. Fama noticed in a 1993 study that over long periods of time, the stocks of smaller companies tend to generate larger returns than those of larger companies.[8]

Real-world investors have been the strongest critics, most notably the famous investor Warren Buffett,* who has publicly criticized the EMH. He claims that good investors search for "discrepancies between the *value* of a business and the *price* of small pieces of that business in the market"—that is, they use the approach known as fundamental analysis.*[9]

> "I'm convinced that there is much inefficiency in the market."
>
> ——Warren Buffett

Responses

Malkiel has always answered challenges to his theory. In 2003, for example, he summarized his responses to all its major critics in an article "The Efficient Market Hypothesis and Its Critics." After listing his critics and explaining their arguments, he examines their investment strategies using empirical* evidence. He claims to show that "these patterns [of their supposedly successful investments] are not robust and dependable in different sample periods."[10] Moreover, he adds that "many of these patterns, even if they did exist, could self-destruct in the future, as many of them have already done."[11]

In other words, once word gets out about a market

irregularity, it disappears. In a way this supports the EMH, since once a market advantage becomes widely known it quickly becomes the norm. Ultimately, Malkiel concludes that, "Our stock markets are far more efficient and far less predictable than some recent academic papers would have us believe"—a position he continues to hold.[12]

As for exceptional investors like Warren Buffett, who "beat the market" year after year, Malkiel takes a measured view. The 11th edition of *Random Walk* suggests that Warren Buffett's success is purely down to luck: "I have become increasingly convinced that the past records of mutual-fund managers are essentially worthless in predicting future success. The few examples of consistently superior performance occur no more frequently than can be expected by chance."[13] This is a very fair point: the random walk is bound to throw up a few long-term winners.

Conflict and Consensus

While the general opinion about the text is positive, the economists Charles P. Kindleberger and Robert Z. Aliber see the EMH as essentially resting on the rational belief that "investors react to changes in economic variables as if they are always fully aware of the long-term implications of each of these changes"— which is impossible.[14] This EMH assumption of "rational behavior" has been persuasively disputed by Kindleberger, Robert J. Shiller,* and others from the field of behavioral economics. Books like *A Non-Random Walk Down Wall Street* provide the empirical evidence to show that stock prices are predictable, and therefore that a bulletproof version of the EMH clearly does not hold.

But a perfectly reliable EMH is not what Malkiel ever really argues exists. *A Random Walk* clearly describes huge, irrational bubbles of the past—from the seventeenth-century Tulip Bulb Craze* in Holland to the subprime mortgage crisis* of the twenty-first century. Although this is not efficient market behavior, the fact that no one can always pinpoint when the market has reached its summit, and that even the cleverest investors sometimes get caught holding onto assets for too long (after their price has fallen considerably), proves the EMH in the longer term. As Malkiel puts it, "While the stock market in the short run may be a voting mechanism, in the long run it is a weighing mechanism. True value will win out in the end. Before the fact, there is no way in which investors can reliably exploit any anomalies or patterns that might exist."

Malkiel is careful to make claims for the EMH only in the long term—something his critics occasionally seem to overlook. Likewise, he maintains that the EMH would only be threatened by the long-term brilliance of a Warren Buffett if you could identify who these successful investors were going to be *before* their market-beating performance, rather than afterward.[15] "There will be some Warren Buffetts in the future," Malkiel admits. "There may be a few of them, but here is the problem: I don't know who they are and I don't think anyone else knows who they are; it's like looking for a needle in the haystack."[16]

1. Jonathan Clarke, et al., "The Efficient Markets Hypothesis", in *Expert Financial Planning: Investment Strategies from Industry Leaders*, ed. Robert C. Arffa (New York: John Wiley & Sons, 2001), 132.

2. Burton G. Malkiel, "The Efficient Market Hypothesis and Its Critics", *Journal of Economic Perspectives* 17, no. 1 (Winter, 2003): 60.

3. Andrew W. Lo and A. Craig MacKinlay, *A Non-Random Walk Down Wall Street* (Princeton; Oxford: Princeton University Press, 1999), 4.

4. Burton G. Malkiel, *A Random Walk Down Wall Street: The Time-Tested Strategy for Successful Investing* (New York: W. W. Norton & Company, 2015), 139.

5. Malkiel, *Random Walk*, 140.

6. Werner F. M. DeBondt and Richard Thaler, "Does the Stock Market Overreact?", *Journal of Finance* 40 (July, 1985): 793.

7. Robert A. Haugen and Josef Lakonishok, *The Incredible January Effect: The Stock Market's Unsolved Mystery* (Homewood: Dow Jones-Irwin, 1987).

8. Malkiel, "The Efficient Market Hypothesis and Its Critics", 67−8.

9. Warren Buffett, "The Superinvestors of Graham and Doddsville", *The Columbia Business School Magazine* (May 17, 1984): 7.

10. Malkiel, "The Efficient Market Hypothesis and Its Critics", 71.

11. Malkiel, "The Efficient Market Hypothesis and Its Critics", 71.

12. Malkiel, "The Efficient Market Hypothesis and Its Critics", 60.

13. Malkiel, *Random Walk*, 398.

14. Robert Z. Aliber and Charles P. Kinderberger, *Manias, Panics, and Crashes: A History of Financial Crises* (London: Palgrave MacMillan, 2015), 53.

15. Clarke, "The Efficient Markets Hypothesis", 131.

16. Mac Greer, "Beating the Market is Like Believing in Santa Claus", *The Motley Fool*, accessed on November 25, 2014, http://www.fool.com/investing/general/2010/09/16/beating-the-market-is-like-believing-in-santa.aspx.

MODULE 10

THE EVOLVING DEBATE

KEY POINTS

* Although Malkiel's theory that the stock* market will always find the "right" price has become very popular, it is not easy to know if investors overreact or underreact to public news affecting a company's share prices (at least in the short term).

* New studies continue to show that simulations of monkeys throwing darts to pick shares could earn at least as much as many managed investment funds.

* Malkiel's popular intellectual justification for the efficient market hypothesis* (EMH) had a radical effect; although it remains controversial, *A Random Walk* is at the center of the ongoing debate about how the stock market works.

Uses and Problems

Burton G. Malkiel's *A Random Walk Down Wall Street: The Time-Tested Strategy for Successful Investing* was at the forefront of a new movement in investment theory and practice—one that said you could ignore the intelligence and expertise of individual investors and bet on the market itself. Critical to this is the careful definition of the EMH, which says that a stock's price captures all known information about its company at that moment.

But to cite one rising challenge to the EMH: *how* investors generally react to public information can vary widely, and the "crowd" can overreact or underreact to relevant news. When they do, even when a stock price *is* purely driven by news, it is not always affected in the right way. These issues driving swings in market prices fall under the larger issue of irrational behavior in the market, which continues to challenge the EMH in important ways. For example, a sophisticated hedge fund* (a pool of money from different investors managed using high-risk methods) might buy into the rising bubble* of a stock price in order to "ride the momentum" upward and then (hopefully) get out in time. This flies in the face of Malkiel's claim that "smart rational traders will correct any mispricings that might arise from the presence of irrational traders."[1] In other words, according to Malkiel, smart investors will sell any stocks that seem to be rising in value as part of a price bubble, since that bubble could burst at any time, leaving them worse off. But sometimes investors do the opposite for irrational reasons, like greed.

> "The literature on the evidence for this [Random Walk] theory is well developed and includes work of the highest quality. Therefore, whether or not we ultimately agree with it, we must at least take the efficient market theory seriously."
> —— Robert J. Shiller, *Irrational Exuberance*

Schools of Thought

Over 40 years on, *A Random Walk* remains one of the most frequently cited investment books. There continue to be large numbers of securities* analysts, academics, and other investors who have either been influenced by it, or have been forced to confront it in promoting a different approach.

A *Random Walk* did not create a school of thought so much

as reflect one: the rising tide of academics and investors who were beginning to question the performance of mutual fund managers, especially considering the high fees such managers typically charge. Citing the EMH, Malkiel's book famously claims that a blindfolded monkey throwing darts at a newspaper's financial pages can select stocks just as well as "experts."[2] The book can be seen as a challenge thrown at mutual fund* managers: "A monkey can do better than you."[3]

This monkey image has now taken on a life of its own. In 2014, the respected financial journal the *Economist* profiled several serious studies inspired by *A Random Walk*.[4] In separate experiments, two research groups, one in California and one at a London business school, tested the performance of fund managers against simulated monkeys throwing darts at the financial pages.[5] Their conclusions were that Malkiel was being too modest: "Simulating a dart-throwing monkey has resulted in portfolios* that would not just beat many investors, but also outperform the market."[6]

In Current Scholarship

These recent "monkey" studies reflect just how central Malkiel's book remains to discussions about how stock markets function, and demonstrate that the essential debate has not moved on that much. "Passive" index mutual funds* contain a broad portfolio of stocks to mirror the returns of the overall stock market. Over the long term, these continue to do well against more "actively" managed mutual funds—especially when the high manager fees, transaction fees, and capital gains tax* are factored in.

That said, a great deal of academic work continues to be done on the EMH, which includes asking the basic question as to how it compares to other investment strategies. Recent books *Principles of Corporate Finance* and *Financial Markets and Institutions* present the ongoing scholarly discussion about what exactly market efficiency* *is* (in terms of the EMH ideal).[7] Just how important the EMH is within today's world of investment and financial theory is another area of debate. Robert J. Shiller* won the 2013 Nobel Prize in Economics for his work on irrational behavior in markets, and ended up, uncomfortably, sharing the prize that year with Eugene F. Fama,* father of the EMH. Afterward, Shiller publicly repeated his opinion that the EMH is a "half-truth."[8]

Yet even recently, extensive data-based research continues to confirm the EMH when applied to the returns of individual companies and relevant indices[9] (that is, lists of companies). Nonetheless, the debate remains complicated: while the approach known as technical analysis* remains unpopular among academics (who see it as unprofitable), it is still widely applied by professionals. Some have suggested that the methods of technical analysis are not applied at their best when used in academic research.[10] Or it could be a delusion common to the world of investment, with money managers fooling themselves into believing it works, as Malkiel repeatedly argues in *A Random Walk*.

The economist Nassim Nicholas Taleb,* with his popular book *The Black Swan: The Impact of the Highly Improbable*

(2007), could be seen as one of Malkiel's main successors. For Taleb, a successful financial manager in his own right, randomness is the determining factor not only in the stock market but also more generally. He claims that it is the highly improbable, highly impactful events that shape the world as we know it; but our reaction is to pretend that this randomness does not exist.[11] He goes on to explore the wider, psychological* human need to see the future as resembling the past. He points out that such understanding can provide a real financial edge, as it allows investors to protect themselves from the damage of destructive market events like the stock market crash of 2007−2008.* Taleb sees the crash as "the result of fragility in systems built in ignorance" of the serious consequences of acting on uncertainty.[12]

1. Burton G. Malkiel, *A Random Walk Down Wall Street: The Time-Tested Strategy for Successful Investing* (New York: W. W. Norton & Company, 2015), 230.

2. Malkiel, *Random Walk*, 26.

3. Malkiel, *Random Walk*, 19.

4. S. H., "No Monkey Business?", *Economist*, June 4, 2014, accessed on November 27, 2015, http://www.economist.com/blogs/freeexchange/2014/06/financial-knowledge-and-investment-performance.

5. Robert D. Arnott, et al., "The Surprising Alpha from Malkie's Monkey and Upside-Down Strategies", *The Journal of Portfolio Management* 39, no. 4 (Summer, 2013); and Andrew Clare, et al., "An Evaluation of Alternative Equity Indices, Part 1", Cass Business School, City University London, March 2013, accessed on January 10, 2016, http://www.cassknowledge.com/sites/default/files/article-attachments/evaluation-alternative-equity-indices-part-1-cass-knowledge.pdf.

6. S. H., "No Monkey Business?".

7. F. Allen, et al., *Principles of Corporate Finance* (New York: McGraw-Hill/Irwin, 2011), 314−320; G. Eakins and S. Mishkin, *Financial Markets and Institutions* (Boston: Prentice Hall, 2012), 117−130.

8. Robert J. Shiller, "Sharing Nobel Honors, and Agreeing to Disagree", *The New York Times*, accessed

on 12 January, 2016, http://www.nytimes.com/2013/10/27/business/sharing-nobel-honors-and-agreeing-to-disagree.html?hp&_r=0.

9. R. W. Parks and E. Zivot, "Financial market efficiency and its implications", *University of Washington, Investment, Capital and Finance*, accessed on 12 January, 2016, http://faculty.washington.edu/ezivot/econ422/Market%20Efficiency%20EZ.pdf.

10. Augustas Degutis and Lina Novickyte, "The Efficient Market Hypothesis: A Critical Review of Literature and Methodology", *Ekonomika* 93, no. 2 (2014): 12.

11. Nassim Nicholas Taleb, *The Black Swan: The Impact of the Highly Improbable* (London: Penguin, 2007), xxii.

12. Taleb, *The Black Swan*, 321.

IMPACT AND INFLUENCE TODAY

KEY POINTS

* Although investing has changed considerably, with the emergence of new theories and complex mathematical approaches in the decades since the first edition of *A Random Walk* was published in 1973, Malkiel claims that in long-term investments, finance professionals can still not perform better than "blindfolded monkeys".

* While the new models seek to exploit small stock* price inefficiencies to make profits, once fund managers' fees have been factored in the results are no better than those achieved by (passive) index funds.*

* Many academics and investors remain determined to prove that there *are* inefficiencies in the market to be consistently exploited by "experts", and therefore to disprove the efficient market hypothesis* (EMH).

Position

Over 40 years since its first publication, Burton G. Malkiel's *A Random Walk Down Wall Street: The Time-Tested Strategy for Successful Investing* remains a vital read for anyone interested in how the stock market works, or anyone looking to invest money in stocks. Its continued popularity suggests that, even while waves of skeptics continue to challenge its basic conclusion, Malkiel's book remains not only important but also persuasive.

These were decades that saw great economic change. The financial services industry* exploded in the United States, offering a new range of sophisticated strategies that all promised to "beat the market" (that is, to provide better earnings than the average increase in the value of stock market shares). These various approaches have had to address the efficient market hypothesis in general and Malkiel's book in particular. That a Wall Street fund manager could invest money better than a monkey was seen as a given before the first edition of *A Random Walk*. Since its publication, the abilities of investing professionals have been seriously challenged—threatening their generous earnings in the process.

The last four decades have also seen a revolution in statistical analysis,* and as a result, the ability to predict behavior through algorithms (a set of rules for solving mathematical problems) and other mathematical tools. Naturally these developments have been applied to making money via the stock market. As a result, quantitative analysts* (known as "quants") who try to predict market movements through mathematical equations, have become more important. Money managers use these new methods of analysis to try to prove that stock markets are predictable, and so pose a direct challenge to *A Random Walk* and the EMH.

> "A tremendous battle is going on, and it's fought with deadly intent because the stakes are tenure for the academics and bonuses for the professionals. That's why I think you'll enjoy this random walk down Wall Street. It has all the ingredients of high drama—including fortunes made and lost and classic arguments about their cause."
>
> —— Burton G. Malkiel, *A Random Walk Down Wall Street*

Interaction

It is fair to say that many investment managers and academic theorists who take an "active" approach (believing they can beat the market by strategically buying and selling stocks) have a clear interest in disproving the EMH. An academic victory over the hypothesis would be valuable to Wall Street, restoring some public trust in the wisdom of mutual fund managers (suggesting that they are at least better than monkeys).

In the past few decades, a steady stream of new—often complicated—academic books have claimed that there are indeed exploitable inefficiencies in the market—such as very hard-to-see "trends" that can be used to predict price movements. In the 11th edition of *Random Walk*, Malkiel is happy to admit this point: "The stock market does not conform perfectly to the mathematician's ideal of the complete independence of present price movements from those of the past."[1] But he maintains that "the systematic relationships that exist are often so small that they are not useful to investors."[2]

In the investment world, very few investors have used strategies that have beaten the market regularly over time. In the 11th edition of *Random Walk*, Malkiel claims that he harbors increasing doubts regarding even this select company: "In previous editions of this book, I provided the names of several investment managers who had enjoyed long-term records of successful portfolio management as well as brief biographies explaining their investment styles ... I have abandoned that practice in the current edition."[3] Malkiel has gradually grown ever more convinced that such success is simply due to chance.[4]

The Continuing Debate

Not only has the debate around Malkiel and the random walk theory failed to advance significantly over the past 40 years, Malkiel's responses to his challengers have not changed much either. Competition is so intense among fund managers, as each bids various stock prices closer to their true value, that it is almost impossible to outperform the market average over time. News gets factored into prices too quickly. Meanwhile, the generally good long-term performances of "passive" funds remain better than the performance of "active" funds, and cutting-edge equations have proven that small inefficiencies in the market are basically insignificant—they cannot produce higher earnings than the stock market average. The same goes for the advancing field of behavioral finance:* until these insights can translate into superior returns for investors over the long term, they cannot prove better than the EMH, in Malkiel's eyes.

That is not to say that behavioral finance is not impressive and developing fast—even Malkiel's latest edition of *A Random Walk* praises the insights and promise of the field—but in the end, the question is one of achieving higher returns over the long term. This practical focus on real investors is another reason for the enduring popularity of *A Random Walk.* As one commentator has put it, "Strictly speaking the EMH is false, but in spirit is profoundly true."[5] That is to say, in the short term there will always be bubbles,* wildly mispriced stocks and all sorts of irrational investor behavior, which would seem to disprove the EMH. But in the long term, empirical* data supports the position that bubbles will always burst, and prices will adjust to a (reasonably) accurate level. The long-term investor can depend on that to make money.

---

1. Burton G. Malkiel, *A Random Walk Down Wall Street: The Time-Tested Strategy for Successful Investing*, (New York: W. W. Norton & Company, 2015), 139.
2. Malkiel, *Random Walk*, 140.
3. Malkiel, *Random Walk*, 398.
4. Malkiel, *Random Walk*, 398.
5. Martin Sewell, "History of the Efficient Market Hypothesis", *UCL Research Note* 11, no. 4 (January 20, 2011): 1.

MODULE 12
WHERE NEXT?

KEY POINTS

* While it is likely that *A Random Walk* will continue to be highly relevant, the financial crash of 2007–2008* has thrown almost every economic belief into serious question and could also impact this book.

* *A Random Walk* will continue to affect conversations about price movements in the stock* market, even if the stock market itself is clearly entering a new, unpredictable era.

* The book is still one of the most cited and frequently mentioned texts in investment theory and practice, and has been for over 40 years; its influence, and the challenge it presents to "active" mutual fund managers, remains as strong as ever.

Potential

It seems likely that Burton G. Malkiel's *A Random Walk Down Wall Street: The Time-Tested Strategy for Successful Investing* will be a well-regarded and popular book about the stock market for years to come. Responses from top-notch investors and academics both to this work, and to the efficient market hypothesis* (EMH) that it promotes, are bound to be ongoing. Many first-time investors will continue reading it in large numbers, absorbing its clear and accessible message.

That said, the state of most stock markets around the world (and the slowdown in the global economy generally) caused Malkiel to end his 11th edition with a cautionary note. He categorizes the post-Internet bubble* era of 2000 onwards as "The

Age of Disenchantment", when "investors were again reminded that the world was a very risky place".[1] While there have been strong returns for investors over the past five years, particularly in the US stock market, this has largely been caused by a policy of "quantitative easing"* (the policy of printing cash and pumping it into the economy, raising the prices of most assets, especially stocks).

How such dramatic intervention by the federal government changes the basic dynamics of the stock market, and perhaps makes rising prices more predictable, is never addressed by Malkiel, which seems curious. He makes the prediction that "we are likely to be in a low-return environment for some time to come"[2] but does not speculate on how the earth-shaking effects of the US subprime mortgage crisis* might deeply change how the stock markets work. To imply that the stock market will function as it did from 1945– 2008 may be a risky guess.

> "It would be unrealistic to anticipate that the generous returns earned by stock market investors during the 2009– 2014 period can be expected during the years ahead."
> —— Burton G. Malkiel, *A Random Walk Down Wall Street*

Future Directions

The core message of *A Random Walk* is that the world of investment is so competitive that no one has a long-term inside edge; so the movements of stock prices are totally unpredictable. This theory is likely to remain influential in the future even without the help of further research. New challenges from areas like behavioral finance* will continue to arise, but unless these rival schools of thought reveal a reliable way to "beat the market", they are unlikely to dislodge the importance of the EMH and Malkiel's popular text.

That said, *A Random Walk* does see price bubbles as short-term mistakes in pricings that get corrected in the longer term: the market itself pops them, and prices fall sharply. This may be true, but specialties like behavioral finance are needed to reveal just how such asset bubbles can get out of control, as happened during the US subprime mortgage crisis.*The then-chairman of the Federal Reserve* (America's central bank), Alan Greenspan,* took the view—both before and after the crash—that asset bubbles in the stock market and housing market need to be left alone to "pop" on their own.[3] In doing so he—like Malkiel and practically every other economist—had no idea about the huge financial structure that had been built on top of the housing bubble of the early 2000s. When it did finally pop, the flood of knock-on effects almost destroyed the entire economy.

A great deal of new theory and analysis is needed to ensure that this does not happen again. While the random walk theory* may be valid for understanding stock prices in normal conditions, it cannot protect the market against another disaster of this kind.

Summary

A Random Walk continues to educate the public about (or against) investment managers who claim to have privileged knowledge about the stock market. Malkiel's text discredits such promises in a convincing way by giving statistical examinations of popular "market-beating" strategies, undermining them further through the straightforward, gimmick-free logic of the EMH. For anyone planning to study investment or to invest in the stock market, *A Random Walk* remains essential reading.

Besides bringing together the major points of the EMH in a highly readable text, and attacking the idea that anyone can regularly "beat the market", Malkiel also shows a positive way forward for the investor. His recommendation that people buy and hold a broad-based index mutual fund* remains good advice—advice that people are taking. As he states in the 11th edition of *A Random Walk*, "During 2014, about one-third of the money invested by individuals and institutions was invested in index funds. And that percentage continues to grow."[4] Despite the system-wide crisis of the 2007–2008 crash, Malkiel still firmly maintains that his time-tested strategy can meet an investor's needs in an uncertain future: "If you will follow the simple rules and timeless lessons espoused in this book, you are likely to do just fine, even during the toughest times."[5]

---

1. Burton G. Malkiel, *A Random Walk Down Wall Street: The Time-Tested Strategy for Successful Investing* (New York: W. W. Norton & Company, 2015), 344.

2. Malkiel, *Random Walk*, 348.

3. For Greenspan's view both before and after the crash, see Alan Greenspan, "Greenspan's Bubble

Bath", *Economist,* September 5, 2002, accessed February 19, 2016, http://www.economist.com/node/1314051; and "Alan Greenspan: The Fed Can't Prevent Market Bubbles", NewsMax Finance, July 24, 2014, accessed February 19, 2016, http://www.newsmax.com/Finance/StreetTalk/alan-greenspan-federal-reserve-bubbles-economy/2014/07/24/id/584744/.

4. Malkiel, *Random Walk,* 181.
5. Malkiel, *Random Walk,* 411.

━◆⋑━ GLOSSARY OF TERMS ━⋐◆━

1. **American Finance Association:** publisher of the *Journal of Finance*, the AFA is an organization founded on the scholarship of financial economics (knowledge of which it seeks to promote).

2. **Behavioral finance:** a field of finance studies exploring the psychological characteristics of people participating in the market, seeking to explain market movements and, in particular, repeated irrational errors.

3. **Bubble:** a conspicuous overpricing of assets.

4. **Capital-asset pricing model:** a model that claims that you must increase the total level of risk in a portfolio to earn superior returns.

5. **Capital gains tax:** tax on the increase in the value of shares (capital) that an investor must pay when selling those shares for more than was originally paid for them.

6. **Closed-end fund:** a fund that raises its capital only once by issuing a fixed number of shares; the price of these closed-end shares is not only a reflection of the assets the fund possesses and manages, but of how many investors want to buy shares in it at the time.

7. **Dow Jones Industrial Average:** a price-weighted average of 30 stocks traded on the NewYork stock exchange and the Nasdaq (the second-largest US stock exchange after NewYork), compiled to measure the performance of the industrial sector of the American economy.

8. **Economics:** the social science describing the production, distribution, and consumption of scarce resources in a world of unlimited wants.

9. **Efficiency:** in the discipline of economics, this is a state where all resources are optimally allocated. In the stock exchange, it means a stock price that comes closest to the true value of the company in which it represents ownership.

10. **Efficient market hypothesis (EMH):** the idea that asset prices, including stock prices, capture all available information about that asset or respective company.

11. **Empirical:** relating to information verifiable by observation, and the

conclusions based on that information, rather than on theory.

12. **Federal Reserve:** the central bank of the United States that regulates the nation's monetary and financial systems.

13. **Financial crash of 2007–2008:** an event that triggered the biggest worldwide decline since the Great Depression of the 1930s. It was caused by the rapid growth in overpriced securities tied to a very risky housing market (especially in the United States). The crash saw many billions of dollars lost on stock markets around the world.

14. **Financial services industry:** the economic services provided by a broad range of businesses in a given country. These include banks, insurance companies, credit unions, real estate companies, and so forth.

15. **Fundamental analysis:** a method of evaluating a security, such as a bond or stock share, by measuring its "intrinsic value"—what it is really worth in the market as opposed to how it is currently priced.

16. **Global economic recession of 2007–2009:** the biggest worldwide decline since the Great Depression of the 1930s. It was triggered by the rapid growth in securities tied to the subprime (highly risky) housing market, especially in the United States. When this collapsed, it caused the bankruptcy of major financial institutions around the world, and government bail-outs to prevent greater chaos.

17. **Great Depression:** a catastrophic economic downturn that began in the United States in the 1920s, soon spreading to Europe, notably Great Britain, and continuing into the 1930s.

18. **Hedge fund:** a pool of money collected from a group of investors and then managed by a general partner, who aims to maximize investor returns whether the market climbs or declines. Hedge funds often use high-risk methods, such as investing with borrowed money.

19. **Index fund/index mutual fund:** a portfolio of diverse stocks, intentionally selected to provide broad market exposure and allow the performance of a portfolio to mirror that of the overall stock market.

20. **Insider information:** non-public information about the state of a publicly traded company. Such information typically gives an advantage to buyers and sellers of that company's stock. Using insider information in this way is illegal.

21. **Initial public offering (IPO):** the first time a privately owned company issues shares and sells them to the public. The company will also call this moment "going public".

22. **Modern portfolio theory:** an attempt to maximize the return (earnings) of a portfolio of stocks, bonds, or other assets. It attempts to minimize the risks by choosing various assets whose risks offset each other.

23. **Mutual fund:** a pool of money collected from a group of investors used to purchase various securities such as stocks and bonds, the profits of which the investors share in proportion to the amount of money each has contributed.

24. **New York stock exchange:** a market where various companies are publicly listed in order to ease trading with investors. It is located in NewYork City and is the largest stock exchange in the world.

25. **Ponzi scheme:** a fraud whereby high rates of return are promised to investors, with little risk. The returns are paid to investors from the money provided by new investors. As long as more new investors enter the scheme, earlier investors receive their promised returns. All but the early investors tend to lose their money.

26. **Psychology:** the study of the human mind and behavior.

27. **Quantitative analysis:** the evaluation of financial markets through often-complex mathematical and statistical modeling. This method seeks to turn mass amounts of information about a market into insight about how it will perform in the future.

28. **Quantitative easing:** the policy of printing cash and pumping it into the economy, raising the prices of most assets, especially stocks.

29. **Random walk theory:** a financial theory that states prices cannot be predicted, because future price movements bear no relation to past price

movements. Such an idea is closely related to the efficient market hypothesis.

30. **Randomness:** a complete lack of predictability of events or sequences.

31. **Security:** a financial agreement showing ownership in a publicly traded corporation (stock) or a promise of repayment for a loan to a governmental body or a corporation (bond).

32. **"Smart beta" strategies:** investment schemes that create an index of purchased stocks, seeking to take advantage of perceived systematic biases or inefficiencies in the market.

33. **Speculator:** for Malkiel, a speculator is someone who buys stocks hoping for a short-term gain.

34. **Stocks:** securities that provide a share of ownership in a corporation and therefore a claim on its future assets and earnings.

35. **Subprime real estate market:** the lower end of the housing market, involving those who are least able to afford to pay their mortgages. Investment in the subprime real estate market is therefore particularly risky.

36. **Systemic risk:** refers to the risk that an entire financial market or entire financial system will collapse, rather than the risk entailed by investing in one aspect of the overall system, such as a company. Investing in a company always exposes you to both forms of risk.

37. **Technical analysis:** a strategy for predicting the future price of securities through the evaluation of past prices and volume, among other statistics.

38. **Tulip Bulb Craze:** a period in seventeenth-century Holland when the contract prices for bulbs of the newly distributed (but still relatively rare) tulips reached astronomical prices, and then collapsed.

39. **Vanguard Group:** a US investment management company that is the largest provider of (primarily index) mutual funds and the second-largest provider or exchange-traded funds in the world as of March 2015. It manages over $3 trillion in assets.

40. **US subprime mortgage crisis:** A 2007–2008 financial crisis in the United Stated that spread globally. It was triggered by a huge fall in real estate prices,

leading to foreclosures, mortgage delinquencies (especially among poorer, "subprime" markets) and eventually sudden insolvencies among large banks and financial firms. Household spending also fell sharply as the world entered a global economic recession.

41. **World War II (1939–1945):** a global conflict fought between the Axis powers (Germany, Italy, and Japan) and the victorious Allied powers (United Kingdom and its colonies, the former Soviet Union, the United States, and others).

◆⟫— PEOPLE MENTIONED IN THE TEXT —⟪◆

1. **Louis Bechelier (1870 −1946)** was a French mathematician. He is often credited with having written the first paper that applied advanced mathematics to the study of finance.

2. **John C. Bogle (1929 −2019)** is an economist and investor from the United States. He is the founder and retired CEO of The Vanguard Group and creator of the first index mutual fund. His book *Common Sense on Mutual Funds* (1999) was a best seller and is considered a classic within the investment community.

3. **Warren Buffett (b. 1930)** is a famous investor. He is the chairman and CEO of the investment fund Berkshire Hathaway, and one of the world's wealthiest people. He credits his successful investment to fundamental analysis, and has publicly questioned the efficient market hypothesis.

4. **Andrea Coombes (b. 1965)** is an award-winning American journalist, personal finance columnist and editor. She sees *A Random Walk Down Wall Street* as one of the most important books for new investors.

5. **Charles D. Ellis (b. 1937)** is an American investment consultant, and believer in index mutual funds. In 1975 he wrote "The Loser's Game" which publicly questioned the performance of nearly every mutual fund manager.

6. **Eugene F. Fama (b. 1939)** is a Nobel Prize-winning economist from the United States whose focus has been the analysis of stock market behavior. He is credited with making the efficient market hypothesis credible through empirical evidence.

7. **Milton Friedman (1912 −2006)** was an American Nobel Prize-winning economist specializing in monetary policy. His theories were particularly influential in the 1980s, and continue to influence conservative economic policy today.

8. **Alan Greenspan (b. 1926)** was the chairman of the Federal Reserve, the US central bank, from 1987 to 2006.

9. **Michael Jensen (b. 1939)** is an American economist and emeritus professor at Harvard University, who specializes in the field of finance.

10. **John Maynard Keynes (1883 −1946)** was an English economist whose macroeconomic theories radically changed the field, and formed the basis for today's "Keynesian school" of economics. He was a believer in technical analysis—that past trends in stock prices could help predict future ones.

11. **Peter Lynch (b. 1944)** is an investor who managed the Magellan Fund from 1977−1990, achieving a 29.2 percent average annual rate of return. He consistently "beat the market."

12. **Paul A. Samuelson (1915−2009)** was the first American to win the Nobel Memorial Prize in Economic Sciences and has been called the "father of modern economics." In the 1970s he publicly questioned the performance of mutual fund managers.

13. **Fred Schwed** was an American stockbroker. He was the author of *Where Are the Customers' Yachts?* (1940), which publicly mocked the value of Wall Street professionals.

14. **Robert J. Shiller (b. 1946)** is a Nobel Prize-winning economist and author of *Irrational Exuberance* (2000). His work in financial economics and behavioral finance is skeptical of the efficient market hypothesis.

15. **George Soros (b. 1930)** is one of the world's wealthiest and most famous investors. He is chairman of Soros Fund Management and an open skeptic of the efficient market hypothesis.

16. **Nassim Nicholas Taleb (b. 1960)** is a Lebanese American author and investor. His work on the nature of randomness and uncertainty has had an impact on the worlds of finance and philosophy, among other disciplines.

WORKS CITED

1. Aliber, Robert Z., and Charles P. Kindleberger. *Manias, Panics, and Crashes: A History of Financial Crises*. Palgrave MacMillan: London, 2015.

2. Allen, Franklin, Richard Brealey, and Stewart Myers. *Principles of Corporate Finance*. McGraw-Hill/Irwin: New York, 2011.

3. Arnott, Robert D., Jason Hsu, Vitali Kalesnik, and Phil Tindall. "The Surprising Alpha from Malkiel's Monkey and Upside-Down Strategies." *Journal of Portfolio Management* 39, no. 4 (summer 2013): 91–105.

4. Buffett, Warren. "2014 Letter to Shareholders." Accessed February 15, 2016. http://www.berkshirehathaway.com/letters/2013ltr.pdf.

5. ____. "The Superinvestors of Graham and Doddsville." *Hermes*, Columbia Business School Magazine (May 17, 1984).

6. Clare, Andrew, Nick Motson, and Steve Thomas. "An Evaluation of Alternative Equity Indices. Part 1: Heuristic and Optimised Weighting Schemes." Cass Business School, City University London, March 2013. Accessed February 15, 2016. http://www.cassknowledge.com/sites/default/files/article-attachments/evaluation-alternative-equity-indices-part–1-cass-knowledge.pdf.

7. Clarke, Jonathan, Tomas Jandik, and Gershon Mandelker. "The Efficient Markets Hypothesis." In *Expert Financial Planning: Investment Strategies from Industry Leaders*, edited by Robert C. Arffa. New York: John Wiley & Sons, 2001.

8. Coombes, Andrea. "Financial Literacy 101: Where to Begin." *The Wall Street Journal*. Accessed February 15, 2016. http://www.wsj.com/articles/SB100014241 27887324556304578117404131372338.

9. DeBondt, Werner F. M., and Richard Thaler. "Does the Stock Market Overreact?" *Journal of Finance* 40, no. 3 (July 1985): 793–805.

10. Degutis, Augustas, and Lina Novickyte, "The Efficient Market Hypothesis: A Critical Review of Literature and Methodology." *Ekonomika* 93, no. 2 (2014).

11. Dunn, Douglas H. *Ponzi*. New York: McGraw-Hill, 1975.

12. Eakins, G., and S. Mishkin. *Financial Markets and Institutions*. Boston: Prentice Hall, 2012.

13. Ellis, Charles D. "The Loser's Game." *Financial Analysts Journal* 31, no. 4 (July/August 1975): 19–26.

14. Fama, Eugene F. "Efficient Markets: A Review of Theory and Empirical Work." *Journal of Finance* 25, no. 2 (May, 1970): 383–417.

15. Friedman, Milton and Anna Jacobson Schwartz. *A Monetary History of the United States, 1867–1960*. Princeton: Princeton University Press, 1963.

16. Greenspan, Alan. "Alan Greenspan: The Fed Can't Prevent Market Bubbles." NewsMax Finance, July 24, 3014. Accessed February 19, 2016. http://www.newsmax.com/Finance/StreetTalk/alan-greenspan-federal-reserve-bubbles-economy/2014/07/24/id/584744/.

17. ____. "Greenspan's Bubble Bath." *Economist*, September 5, 2002. Accessed February 19, 2016. http://www.economist.com/node/1314051.

18. Greer, Mac. "Beating the Market is Like Believing in Santa Claus." *The Motley Fool*, September 16, 2010. Accessed February 16, 2016. http://www.fool.com/investing/general/2010/09/16/beating-the-market-is-like-believing-in-santa.aspx.

19. H. S. "No Monkey Business?" *Economist*, June 4, 2014. Accessed February 16, 2016. http://www.economist.com/blogs/freeexchange/2014/06/financial-knowledge-and-investment-performance.

20. Keynes, John Maynard. *The General Theory of Employment, Interest and Money*. London: Macmillan, 1936.

21. Krugman, Paul and Robin Wells. "The Busts Keep Getting Bigger: Why?" *New York Review of Books*, July 14, 2011.

22. Lo, Andrew W., and A. Craig MacKinlay. *A Non-Random Walk Down Wall Street*. Princeton; Oxford: Princeton University Press, 1999.

23. Majouji, Ramy. "The Financial Markets Context." Open University OpenLearn. Accessed February 16, 2016. http://www.open.edu/openlearn/money-management/money/accounting-and-finance/the-financial-markets-context/content-section---acknowledgements.

24. Malkiel, Burton G. "The Efficient Market Hypothesis and Its Critics." *Journal of Economic Perspectives* 17, no. 1 (Winter, 2003).

25. ____. *A Random Walk Down Wall Street: The Time-Tested Strategy for Successful Investing*. New York: W. W. Norton & Company, 2015.

26. ____. "The Valuation of Closed-End Investment Company Shares." *Journal of Finance* 32, no. 3 (June 1977): 847–59.

27. *The Motley Fool*. "Investment Greats: Burton Malkiel." Accessed February 16, 2016. http://news.fool.co.uk/news/investing/2011/01/04/investment-greats-burton-malkiel.aspx.

28. Parks, R. W. and Zivot, E. "Financial Market Efficiency and Its Implications." University of Washington Investment, Capital and Finance, 2006. Accessed February 16, 2016. http://faculty.washington.edu/ezivot/econ422/Market%20 Efficiency%20EZ.pdf.

29. Ro, Sam. "Finance Wizard Burton Malkiel Defends the Efficient Market Hypothesis." *Business Insider UK.* Accessed February 16, 2016. http://www. businessinsider.com/burton-malkiel-efficient-market-hypothesis-2012-4?IR=T.

30. Samuelson, Paul A. "Challenge to Judgment." *Journal of Portfolio Management* 1, no. 1 (Fall 1974).

31. Schwed, Fred Jr. *Where Are the Customers' Yachts?* Hoboken, NJ: John Wiley & Sons, 2006.

32. Sewell, Martin. "History of the Efficient Market Hypothesis." *University College London Research Note* 11, no. 4 (January 20, 2011).

33. Shiller, Robert J. *Irrational Exuberance.* Princeton: Princeton University Press, 2000.

34. ____. "Sharing Nobel Honors, and Agreeing to Disagree." *New York Times*, October 26, 2013. Accessed February 16, 2016. http://www.nytimes.com/2013/ 10/27/business/sharing-nobel-honors-and-agreeing-to-disagree.html?hp&_r=0.

35. Soros, George. "Soros: Financial Markets." *Financial Times*, October 27, 2009. Accessed February 19, 2016. http://www.ft.com/intl/cms/s/2/dbc0e0c6-bfe9-11de-aed2-00144feab49a.html#axzz40d8gJIsO

36. Taleb, Nassim Nicholas. *The Black Swan: The Impact of the Highly Improbable.* London: Penguin: 2007.

37. Udland, Myles. "30 Years Ago Warren Buffett Gave Away The Secret To Good Investing And Correctly Predicted No One Would Listen." *Business Insider UK*, August 14, 2014. Accessed February 16, 2015. http://uk. businessinsider.com/ warren-buffett-graham-and-doddsville-lecture-2014-8?r=US&IR=T.

38. Wealthfront company website. Accessed February 16, 2016. https://www. wealthfront.com/our-beliefs.

原书作者简介

伯顿·G.马尔基尔生于1932年,是最具影响力的美国经济学家之一,专门研究股市的运作方式。在哈佛大学取得工商管理硕士学位后,马尔基尔在华尔街一家投资公司工作了几年,之后转战学术界,并获得普林斯顿大学经济学博士学位。他很快成为一名教授,现已结束漫长的职业生涯退休。马尔基尔还担任了多家公司的董事,这使他对学术界和商界都颇具洞察力。他还曾担任美国经济顾问委员会委员,为美国总统提供咨询服务。马尔基尔出版了大量著作和论文,其中以1973年出版的《漫步华尔街》最为知名。

本书作者简介

尼克·伯顿博士获缅因州包德恩学院经济学学位与牛津大学英语文学博士学位。他是一位屡获殊荣的剧作家,创作的主题包罗万象,从金融危机到浪漫主义诗人的生平,无所不有。他目前在伦敦大学皇家霍洛威学院教授戏剧创作,兼任牛津大学沃弗森学院的创意艺术研究员。

世界名著中的批判性思维

《世界思想宝库钥匙丛书》致力于深入浅出地阐释全世界著名思想家的观点,不论是谁、在何处都能了解到,从而推进批判性思维发展。

《世界思想宝库钥匙丛书》与世界顶尖大学的一流学者合作,为一系列学科中最有影响的著作推出新的分析文本,介绍其观点和影响。在这一不断扩展的系列中,每种选入的著作都代表了历经时间考验的思想典范。通过为这些著作提供必要背景、揭示原作者的学术渊源以及说明这些著作所产生的影响,本系列图书希望让读者以新视角看待这些划时代的经典之作。读者应学会思考、运用并挑战这些著作中的观点,而不是简单接受它们。

ABOUT THE AUTHOR OF THE ORIGINAL WORK

Born in 1932, **Burton G. Malkiel** is one of the most influential American economists specializing in how the stock markets work. After earning an MBA at Harvard University, Malkiel worked for a Wall Street investment firm for a couple of years before moving to academia and gaining a PhD in economics from Princeton. He quickly became a professor, and after a long career is now retired. Malkiel has also acted as a director of many companies, giving him a perspective on both the academic and business worlds. He has served as a member of the Council of Economic Advisers, advising the US president. Malkiel has published numerous books and articles, but is best known for 1973's *A Random Walk Down Wall Street*.

ABOUT THE AUTHORS OF THE ANALYSIS

Dr Nick Burton holds a degree in economics from Bowdoin College, Maine, and a DPhil in English literature from Oxford. An award-winning playwright who has taken on subjects as diverse as the financial crisis and the lives of the Romantic poets, he currently lectures on play-writing at Royal Holloway, University of London, and is the Creative Arts Fellow at Wolfson College, Oxford.

ABOUT MACAT
GREAT WORKS FOR CRITICAL THINKING

Macat is focused on making the ideas of the world's great thinkers accessible and comprehensible to everybody, everywhere, in ways that promote the development of enhanced critical thinking skills.

It works with leading academics from the world's top universities to produce new analyses that focus on the ideas and the impact of the most influential works ever written across a wide variety of academic disciplines. Each of the works that sit at the heart of its growing library is an enduring example of great thinking. But by setting them in context — and looking at the influences that shaped their authors, as well as the responses they provoked — Macat encourages readers to look at these classics and game-changers with fresh eyes. Readers learn to think, engage and challenge their ideas, rather than simply accepting them.

批判性思维与《漫步华尔街》

首要批判性思维技巧：评估

次要批判性思维技巧：分析

如何在股票投资上获得良好回报引起的论辩不断，伯顿·G.马尔基尔 1973 年出版的《漫步华尔街》是其中一项轰动性的贡献。自首次出版后，《漫步华尔街》又再版、修改了数次，对投资策略界来说至今仍是不可或缺，但也继续引发投资专家的争论。

《漫步华尔街》的核心是一个简单的评估问题：投资专家到底有多成功？金融界一直充斥着声称拥有超越市场的知识和专长，并因此能为投资者谋取较高收益的人。但马尔基尔提问，他们究竟真的有多成功？通过仔细评估"技术分析派"和"基本面分析派"的业绩表现，马尔基尔证明，许多鼓吹分析师的成功的说法并不足信。他发现，主要的主动投资策略都存在缺陷。虽然主动管理基金在某一年收益可观，但都似乎不可避免地在随后的几年里跌破平均水平。通过评估中长期数据，马尔基尔发现，主动管理基金的平均收益比被动跟踪整体市场指数的基金要差得多。

虽然许多投资专业人士仍在反驳马尔基尔的重大发现，但马尔基尔对吹捧专业投资者的各种论断的优劣逐一剖析，有力地证明了自己的被动策略胜出。

CRITICAL THINKING AND *A RANDOM WALK DOWN WALL STREET*

- Primary critical thinking skill: EVALUATION
- Secondary critical thinking skill: ANAYLSIS

Burton G. Malkiel's 1973 *A Random Walk Down Wall Street* was an explosive contribution to debates about how to reap a good return on investing in stocks and shares. Reissued and updated many times since, Malkiel's text remains an indispensable contribution to the world of investment strategy—one that continues to cause controversy among investment professionals today.

At the book's heart lies a simple question of evaluation: just how successful are investment experts? The financial world was, and is, full of people who claim to have the knowledge and expertise to outperform the markets, and produce larger gains for investors as a result of their knowledge. But how successful, Malkiel asked, are they really? Via careful evaluations of performance—looking at those who invested via 'technical analysis' and 'fundamental analysis'— he was able to challenge the adequacy of many of the claims made for analysts' success. Malkiel found the major active investment strategies to be significantly flawed. Where actively managed funds posted big gains one year, they seemingly inevitably posted below average gains in succeeding years. By evaluating the figures over the medium and long term, indeed, Malkiel discovered that actively-managed funds did far worse on average than those that passively followed the general market index.

Though many investment professionals still argue against Malkiel's influential findings, his exploration of the strengths and weaknesses of the argument for believing investors' claims provides strong evidence that his own passive strategy wins out overall.

《世界思想宝库钥匙丛书》简介

《世界思想宝库钥匙丛书》致力于为一系列在各领域产生重大影响的人文社科类经典著作提供独特的学术探讨。每一本读物都不仅仅是原经典著作的内容摘要，而是介绍并深入研究原经典著作的学术渊源、主要观点和历史影响。这一丛书的目的是提供一套学习资料，以促进读者掌握批判性思维，从而更全面、深刻地去理解重要思想。

每一本读物分为 3 个部分：学术渊源、学术思想和学术影响，每个部分下有 4 个小节。这些章节旨在从各个方面研究原经典著作及其反响。

由于独特的体例，每一本读物不但易于阅读，而且另有一项优点：所有读物的编排体例相同，读者在进行某个知识层面的调查或研究时可交叉参阅多本该丛书中的相关读物，从而开启跨领域研究的路径。

为了方便阅读，每本读物最后还列出了术语表和人名表（在书中则以星号＊标记），此外还有参考文献。

《世界思想宝库钥匙丛书》与剑桥大学合作，理清了批判性思维的要点，即如何通过 6 种技能来进行有效思考。其中 3 种技能让我们能够理解问题，另 3 种技能让我们有能力解决问题。这 6 种技能合称为"批判性思维 PACIER 模式"，它们是：

分析：了解如何建立一个观点；

评估：研究一个观点的优点和缺点；

阐释：对意义所产生的问题加以理解；

创造性思维：提出新的见解，发现新的联系；

解决问题：提出切实有效的解决办法；

理性化思维：创建有说服力的观点。

THE MACAT LIBRARY

The Macat Library is a series of unique academic explorations of seminal works in the humanities and social sciences — books and papers that have had a significant and widely recognised impact on their disciplines. It has been created to serve as much more than just a summary of what lies between the covers of a great book. It illuminates and explores the influences on, ideas of, and impact of that book. Our goal is to offer a learning resource that encourages critical thinking and fosters a better, deeper understanding of important ideas.

Each publication is divided into three Sections: Influences, Ideas, and Impact. Each Section has four Modules. These explore every important facet of the work, and the responses to it.

This Section-Module structure makes a Macat Library book easy to use, but it has another important feature. Because each Macat book is written to the same format, it is possible (and encouraged!) to cross-reference multiple Macat books along the same lines of inquiry or research. This allows the reader to open up interesting interdisciplinary pathways.

To further aid your reading, lists of glossary terms and people mentioned are included at the end of this book (these are indicated by an asterisk [*] throughout) — as well as a list of works cited.

Macat has worked with the University of Cambridge to identify the elements of critical thinking and understand the ways in which six different skills combine to enable effective thinking.

Three allow us to fully understand a problem; three more give us the tools to solve it. Together, these six skills make up the PACIER model of critical thinking. They are:

ANALYSIS — understanding how an argument is built
EVALUATION — exploring the strengths and weaknesses of an argument
INTERPRETATION — understanding issues of meaning
CREATIVE THINKING — coming up with new ideas and fresh connections
PROBLEM-SOLVING — producing strong solutions
REASONING — creating strong arguments

"《世界思想宝库钥匙丛书》提供了独一无二的跨学科学习和研究工具。它介绍那些革新了各自学科研究的经典著作，还邀请全世界一流专家和教育机构进行严谨的分析，为每位读者打开世界顶级教育的大门。"

—— 安德烈亚斯·施莱歇尔，
经济合作与发展组织教育与技能司司长

"《世界思想宝库钥匙丛书》直面大学教育的巨大挑战……他们组建了一支精干而活跃的学者队伍，来推出在研究广度上颇具新意的教学材料。"

—— 布罗尔斯教授、勋爵，剑桥大学前校长

"《世界思想宝库钥匙丛书》的愿景令人赞叹。它通过分析和阐释那些曾深刻影响人类思想以及社会、经济发展的经典文本，提供了新的学习方法。它推动批判性思维，这对于任何社会和经济体来说都是至关重要的。这就是未来的学习方法。"

—— 查尔斯·克拉克阁下，英国前教育大臣

"对于那些影响了各自领域的著作，《世界思想宝库钥匙丛书》能让人们立即了解到围绕那些著作展开的评论性言论，这让该系列图书成为在这些领域从事研究的师生们不可或缺的资源。"

—— 威廉·特朗佐教授，加利福尼亚大学圣地亚哥分校

"Macat offers an amazing first-of-its-kind tool for interdisciplinary learning and research. Its focus on works that transformed their disciplines and its rigorous approach, drawing on the world's leading experts and educational institutions, opens up a world-class education to anyone."

—— Andreas Schleicher, Director for Education and Skills, Organisation for Economic Co-operation and Development

"Macat is taking on some of the major challenges in university education... They have drawn together a strong team of active academics who are producing teaching materials that are novel in the breadth of their approach."

—— Prof Lord Broers, former Vice-Chancellor of the University of Cambridge

"The Macat vision is exceptionally exciting. It focuses upon new modes of learning which analyse and explain seminal texts which have profoundly influenced world thinking and so social and economic development. It promotes the kind of critical thinking which is essential for any society and economy. This is the learning of the future."

—— Rt Hon Charles Clarke, former UK Secretary of State for Education

"The Macat analyses provide immediate access to the critical conversation surrounding the books that have shaped their respective discipline, which will make them an invaluable resource to all of those, students and teachers, working in the field."

—— Prof William Tronzo, University of California at San Diego

The Macat Library
世界思想宝库钥匙丛书

TITLE	中文书名	类别
An Analysis of Arjun Appadurai's *Modernity at Large: Cultural Dimensions of Globalisation*	解析阿尔君·阿帕杜莱《消失的现代性：全球化的文化维度》	人类学
An Analysis of Claude Lévi-Strauss's *Structural Anthropology*	解析克劳德·列维-斯特劳斯《结构人类学》	人类学
An Analysis of Marcel Mauss's *The Gift*	解析马塞尔·莫斯《礼物》	人类学
An Analysis of Jared M. Diamond's *Guns, Germs, and Steel: The Fate of Human Societies*	解析贾雷德·戴蒙德《枪炮、病菌与钢铁：人类社会的命运》	人类学
An Analysis of Clifford Geertz's *The Interpretation of Cultures*	解析克利福德·格尔茨《文化的解释》	人类学
An Analysis of Philippe Ariès's *Centuries of Childhood: A Social History of Family Life*	解析菲力浦·阿利埃斯《儿童的世纪：旧制度下的儿童和家庭生活》	人类学
An Analysis of W. Chan Kim & Renée Mauborgne's *Blue Ocean Strategy*	解析金伟灿/勒妮·莫博涅《蓝海战略》	商业
An Analysis of John P. Kotter's *Leading Change*	解析约翰·P.科特《领导变革》	商业
An Analysis of Michael E. Porter's *Competitive Strategy: Techniques for Analyzing Industries and Competitors*	解析迈克尔·E.波特《竞争战略：分析产业和竞争对手的技术》	商业
An Analysis of Jean Lave & Etienne Wenger's *Situated Learning: Legitimate Peripheral Participation*	解析琼·莱夫/艾蒂纳·温格《情境学习：合法的边缘性参与》	商业
An Analysis of Douglas McGregor's *The Human Side of Enterprise*	解析道格拉斯·麦格雷戈《企业的人性面》	商业
An Analysis of Milton Friedman's *Capitalism and Freedom*	解析米尔顿·弗里德曼《资本主义与自由》	商业
An Analysis of Ludwig von Mises's *The Theory of Money and Credit*	解析路德维希·冯·米塞斯《货币和信用理论》	经济学
An Analysis of Adam Smith's *The Wealth of Nations*	解析亚当·斯密《国富论》	经济学
An Analysis of Thomas Piketty's *Capital in the Twenty-First Century*	解析托马斯·皮凯蒂《21世纪资本论》	经济学
An Analysis of Nassim Nicholas Taleb's *The Black Swan: The Impact of the Highly Improbable*	解析纳西姆·尼古拉斯·塔勒布《黑天鹅：如何应对不可预知的未来》	经济学
An Analysis of Ha-Joon Chang's *Kicking Away the Ladder*	解析张夏准《富国陷阱：发达国家为何踢开梯子》	经济学
An Analysis of Thomas Robert Malthus's *An Essay on the Principle of Population*	解析托马斯·马萨斯《人口论》	经济学

An Analysis of John Maynard Keynes's *The General Theory of Employment, Interest and Money*	解析约翰·梅纳德·凯恩斯《就业、利息和货币通论》	经济学
An Analysis of Milton Friedman's *The Role of Monetary Policy*	解析米尔顿·弗里德曼《货币政策的作用》	经济学
An Analysis of Burton G. Malkiel's *A Random Walk Down Wall Street*	解析伯顿·G.马尔基尔《漫步华尔街》	经济学
An Analysis of Friedrich A. Hayek's *The Road to Serfdom*	解析弗里德里希·A.哈耶克《通往奴役之路》	经济学
An Analysis of Charles P. Kindleberger's *Manias, Panics, and Crashes: A History of Financial Crises*	解析查尔斯·P.金德尔伯格《疯狂、惊恐和崩溃：金融危机史》	经济学
An Analysis of Amartya Sen's *Development as Freedom*	解析阿马蒂亚·森《以自由看待发展》	经济学
An Analysis of Rachel Carson's *Silent Spring*	解析蕾切尔·卡森《寂静的春天》	地理学
An Analysis of Charles Darwin's *On the Origin of Species: by Means of Natural Selection, or The Preservation of Favoured Races in the Struggle for Life*	解析查尔斯·达尔文《物种起源》	地理学
An Analysis of World Commission on Environment and Development's *The Brundtland Report, Our Common Future*	解析世界环境与发展委员会《布伦特兰报告：我们共同的未来》	地理学
An Analysis of James E. Lovelock's *Gaia: A New Look at Life on Earth*	解析詹姆斯·E.拉伍洛克《盖娅：地球生命的新视野》	地理学
An Analysis of Paul Kennedy's *The Rise and Fall of the Great Powers: Economic Change and Military Conflict from 1500—2000*	解析保罗·肯尼迪《大国的兴衰：1500—2000 年的经济变革与军事冲突》	历史
An Analysis of Janet L. Abu-Lughod's *Before European Hegemony: The World System A. D. 1250—1350*	解析珍妮特·L.阿布–卢格霍德《欧洲霸权之前：1250—1350 年的世界体系》	历史
An Analysis of Alfred W. Crosby's *The Columbian Exchange: Biological and Cultural Consequences of 1492*	解析艾尔弗雷德·W.克罗斯比《哥伦布大交换：1492 年以后的生物影响和文化冲击》	历史
An Analysis of Tony Judt's *Postwar: A History of Europe since 1945*	解析托尼·朱特《战后欧洲史》	历史
An Analysis of Richard J. Evans's *In Defence of History*	解析理查德·J.艾文斯《捍卫历史》	历史
An Analysis of Eric Hobsbawm's *The Age of Revolution: Europe 1789–1848*	解析艾瑞克·霍布斯鲍姆《革命的年代：欧洲 1789—1848 年》	历史

An Analysis of Roland Barthes's *Mythologies*	解析罗兰·巴特《神话学》	文学与批判理论
An Analysis of Simon de Beauvoir's *The Second Sex*	解析西蒙娜·德·波伏娃《第二性》	文学与批判理论
An Analysis of Edward W. Said's *Orientalism*	解析爱德华·W. 萨义德《东方主义》	文学与批判理论
An Analysis of Virginia Woolf's *A Room of One's Own*	解析弗吉尼亚·伍尔芙《一间自己的房间》	文学与批判理论
An Analysis of Judith Butler's *Gender Trouble*	解析朱迪斯·巴特勒《性别麻烦》	文学与批判理论
An Analysis of Ferdinand de Saussure's *Course in General Linguistics*	解析费尔迪南·德·索绪尔《普通语言学教程》	文学与批判理论
An Analysis of Susan Sontag's *On Photography*	解析苏珊·桑塔格《论摄影》	文学与批判理论
An Analysis of Walter Benjamin's *The Work of Art in the Age of Mechanical Reproduction*	解析瓦尔特·本雅明《机械复制时代的艺术作品》	文学与批判理论
An Analysis of W.E.B. Du Bois's *The Souls of Black Folk*	解析 W.E.B. 杜波依斯《黑人的灵魂》	文学与批判理论
An Analysis of Plato's *The Republic*	解析柏拉图《理想国》	哲学
An Analysis of Plato's *Symposium*	解析柏拉图《会饮篇》	哲学
An Analysis of Aristotle's *Metaphysics*	解析亚里士多德《形而上学》	哲学
An Analysis of Aristotle's *Nicomachean Ethics*	解析亚里士多德《尼各马可伦理学》	哲学
An Analysis of Immanuel Kant's *Critique of Pure Reason*	解析伊曼努尔·康德《纯粹理性批判》	哲学
An Analysis of Ludwig Wittgenstein's *Philosophical Investigations*	解析路德维希·维特根斯坦《哲学研究》	哲学
An Analysis of G.W.F. Hegel's *Phenomenology of Spirit*	解析 G.W.F. 黑格尔《精神现象学》	哲学
An Analysis of Baruch Spinoza's *Ethics*	解析巴鲁赫·斯宾诺莎《伦理学》	哲学
An Analysis of Hannah Arendt's *The Human Condition*	解析汉娜·阿伦特《人的境况》	哲学
An Analysis of G.E.M. Anscombe's *Modern Moral Philosophy*	解析 G.E.M. 安斯康姆《现代道德哲学》	哲学
An Analysis of David Hume's *An Enquiry Concerning Human Understanding*	解析大卫·休谟《人类理解研究》	哲学

An Analysis of Søren Kierkegaard's *Fear and Trembling*	解析索伦·克尔凯郭尔《恐惧与战栗》	哲学
An Analysis of René Descartes's *Meditations on First Philosophy*	解析勒内·笛卡尔《第一哲学沉思录》	哲学
An Analysis of Friedrich Nietzsche's *On the Genealogy of Morality*	解析弗里德里希·尼采《论道德的谱系》	哲学
An Analysis of Gilbert Ryle's *The Concept of Mind*	解析吉尔伯特·赖尔《心的概念》	哲学
An Analysis of Thomas Kuhn's *The Structure of Scientific Revolutions*	解析托马斯·库恩《科学革命的结构》	哲学
An Analysis of John Stuart Mill's *Utilitarianism*	解析约翰·斯图亚特·穆勒《功利主义》	哲学
An Analysis of Aristotle's *Politics*	解析亚里士多德《政治学》	政治学
An Analysis of Niccolò Machiavelli's *The Prince*	解析尼科洛·马基雅维利《君主论》	政治学
An Analysis of Karl Marx's *Capital*	解析卡尔·马克思《资本论》	政治学
An Analysis of Benedict Anderson's *Imagined Communities*	解析本尼迪克特·安德森《想象的共同体》	政治学
An Analysis of Samuel P. Huntington's *The Clash of Civilizations and the Remaking of World Order*	解析塞缪尔·P.亨廷顿《文明的冲突与世界秩序重建》	政治学
An Analysis of Alexis de Tocqueville's *Democracy in America*	解析阿列克西·德·托克维尔《论美国的民主》	政治学
An Analysis of John A. Hobson's *Imperialism: A Study*	解析约翰·A.霍布森《帝国主义》	政治学
An Analysis of Thomas Paine's *Common Sense*	解析托马斯·潘恩《常识》	政治学
An Analysis of John Rawls's *A Theory of Justice*	解析约翰·罗尔斯《正义论》	政治学
An Analysis of Francis Fukuyama's *The End of History and the Last Man*	解析弗朗西斯·福山《历史的终结与最后的人》	政治学
An Analysis of John Locke's *Two Treatises of Government*	解析约翰·洛克《政府论》	政治学
An Analysis of Sun Tzu's *The Art of War*	解析孙武《孙子兵法》	政治学
An Analysis of Henry Kissinger's *World Order: Reflections on the Character of Nations and the Course of History*	解析亨利·基辛格《世界秩序》	政治学
An Analysis of Jean-Jacques Rousseau's *The Social Contract*	解析让-雅克·卢梭《社会契约论》	政治学

An Analysis of Odd Arne Westad's *The Global Cold War: Third World Interventions and the Making of Our Times*	解析文安立《全球冷战：美苏对第三世界的干涉与当代世界的形成》	政治学
An Analysis of Sigmund Freud's *The Interpretation of Dreams*	解析西格蒙德·弗洛伊德《梦的解析》	心理学
An Analysis of William James' *The Principles of Psychology*	解析威廉·詹姆斯《心理学原理》	心理学
An Analysis of Philip Zimbardo's *The Lucifer Effect*	解析菲利普·津巴多《路西法效应》	心理学
An Analysis of Leon Festinger's *A Theory of Cognitive Dissonance*	解析利昂·费斯汀格《认知失调论》	心理学
An Analysis of Richard H. Thaler & Cass R. Sunstein's *Nudge: Improving Decisions about Health, Wealth, and Happiness*	解析理查德·H. 泰勒 / 卡斯·R. 桑斯坦《助推：如何做出有关健康、财富和幸福的更优决策》	心理学
An Analysis of Gordon Allport's *The Nature of Prejudice*	解析高尔登·奥尔波特《偏见的本质》	心理学
An Analysis of Steven Pinker's *The Better Angels of Our Nature: Why Violence Has Declined*	解析斯蒂芬·平克《人性中的善良天使：暴力为什么会减少》	心理学
An Analysis of Stanley Milgram's *Obedience to Authority*	解析斯坦利·米尔格拉姆《对权威的服从》	心理学
An Analysis of Betty Friedan's *The Feminine Mystique*	解析贝蒂·弗里丹《女性的奥秘》	心理学
An Analysis of David Riesman's *The Lonely Crowd: A Study of the Changing American Character*	解析大卫·理斯曼《孤独的人群：美国人社会性格演变之研究》	社会学
An Analysis of Franz Boas's *Race, Language and Culture*	解析弗朗兹·博厄斯《种族、语言与文化》	社会学
An Analysis of Pierre Bourdieu's *Outline of a Theory of Practice*	解析皮埃尔·布尔迪厄《实践理论大纲》	社会学
An Analysis of Max Weber's *The Protestant Ethic and the Spirit of Capitalism*	解析马克斯·韦伯《新教伦理与资本主义精神》	社会学
An Analysis of Jane Jacobs's *The Death and Life of Great American Cities*	解析简·雅各布斯《美国大城市的死与生》	社会学
An Analysis of C. Wright Mills's *The Sociological Imagination*	解析 C. 赖特·米尔斯《社会学的想象力》	社会学
An Analysis of Robert E. Lucas Jr.'s *Why Doesn't Capital Flow from Rich to Poor Countries?*	解析小罗伯特·E. 卢卡斯《为何资本不从富国流向穷国？》	社会学

An Analysis of Émile Durkheim's *On Suicide*	解析埃米尔·迪尔凯姆《自杀论》	社会学
An Analysis of Eric Hoffer's *The True Believer: Thoughts on the Nature of Mass Movements*	解析埃里克·霍弗《狂热分子：群众运动圣经》	社会学
An Analysis of Jared M. Diamond's *Collapse: How Societies Choose to Fail or Survive*	解析贾雷德·M.戴蒙德《大崩溃：社会如何选择兴亡》	社会学
An Analysis of Michel Foucault's *The History of Sexuality Vol. 1: The Will to Knowledge*	解析米歇尔·福柯《性史（第一卷）：求知意志》	社会学
An Analysis of Michel Foucault's *Discipline and Punish*	解析米歇尔·福柯《规训与惩罚》	社会学
An Analysis of Richard Dawkins's *The Selfish Gene*	解析理查德·道金斯《自私的基因》	社会学
An Analysis of Antonio Gramsci's *Prison Notebooks*	解析安东尼奥·葛兰西《狱中札记》	社会学
An Analysis of Augustine's *Confessions*	解析奥古斯丁《忏悔录》	神学
An Analysis of C.S. Lewis's *The Abolition of Man*	解析C.S.路易斯《人之废》	神学

图书在版编目（CIP）数据

解析伯顿·G·马尔基尔《漫步华尔街》/ 尼克·伯顿（Nick Burton）著；
刘积慧译.—上海：上海外语教育出版社，2019
（世界思想宝库钥匙丛书）
ISBN 978-7-5446-5795-2

Ⅰ.①解… Ⅱ.①尼… ②刘… Ⅲ.①股票投资—经验—美国 Ⅳ.①F837.125

中国版本图书馆CIP数据核字（2019）第052261号

This Chinese-English bilingual edition of *An Analysis of Burton G. Malkiel's* A Random Walk
Down Wall Street is published by arrangement with Macat International Limited.
Licensed for sale throughout the world.
本书汉英双语版由Macat国际有限公司授权上海外语教育出版社有限公司出版。
供在全世界范围内发行、销售。

图字：09－2018－549

出版发行：**上海外语教育出版社**
（上海外国语大学内） 邮编：200083
电　　话：021-65425300（总机）
电子邮箱：bookinfo@sflep.com.cn
网　　址：http://www.sflep.com
责任编辑：王　璐

印　　刷：上海市崇明县裕安印刷厂
开　　本：890×1240　1/32　印张 5.75　字数 118千字
版　　次：2019 年 8月第 1版　2019 年 8月第 1次印刷
印　　数：2 100 册

书　　号：ISBN 978-7-5446-5795-2 / F
定　　价：30.00 元
本版图书如有印装质量问题，可向本社调换
质量服务热线：4008-213-263　电子邮箱：**editorial@sflep.com**